Hituzi's Linguistics
Textbook
Series 3

Language Change

R. L. Trask

Japanese Notes by
Iyeiri Yoko

HITUZI SYOBO

LANGUAGE CHANGE by Larry Trask
Copyright ©1994 by R. L. Trask
All Rights Reserved.

Published in Japan by Hituzi Syobo Publishing
Japanese notes by ©IYEIRI Yoko

Reprint rights in the English and all rights in Japanese notes in this book are reserved; no part of this publication may be reproduced, stored in a retrieval system, or transmitted in any form or by any means, electronic, mechanical, photocopying, recording, or otherwise without the prior written permission of the publisher.

This edition published by arrangement with Taylor & Francis Books Ltd, 3 Park Square, Milton Park, Abingdon, Oxon OX14 4RN, UK through The English Agency (Japan) Ltd.

Hituzi Syobo Publishing
Yamato bldg. 2f, 2-1-2 Sengoku Bunkyo-ku Tokyo, Japan
112-0011

Telephone: +81-3-5319-4916
Facsimile: +81-3-5319-4917
e-mail: toiawase@hituzi.co.jp
http://www.hituzi.co.jp/
postal transfer: 00120-8-142852

ISBN978-4-89476-999-1
Printed in Japan

はじめに

著者の Robert Lawrence Trask(1944 年 11 月 10 日−2004 年 3 月 27 日)は、元サセックス大学の言語学教授[1]。歴史言語学およびバスク語を専門領域とし、*Language Change*(1994)の他にも、*A Dictionary of Grammatical Terms in Linguistics*(1993), *Historical Linguistics*(1996), *The History of Basque*(1997)など、多数の著作がある。

Language Change の本文に沿って注釈を付したが、本書の英語は比較的容易であるので、英文解釈のための注釈よりも、本書のテーマである英語の変化についての理解を深めるための注釈に重点を置いた。本書の特徴は、本文をできるだけ簡潔な記述にとどめ、むしろ各ユニットに EXERCISE を配置することで、作業をしながら読者に内容を掘り下げてもらうという構成にある。英語史の入門書には、英語史の専門知識をきれいに整理して提示する、英語の歴史をストーリーとして興味深く語る、ワークブック形式で読者の自主的な気づきを促す、などさまざまな種類のものがあり、本書は最後のグループに属すると言える。ワークブック形式の英語史も一つの伝統をなしていて、他にも Freeborn(1992), *From Old English to Standard English: A Course Book in Language Variation across Time* や Brinton & Arnovick(2006), *The English Language: A Linguistic History* の他、本書と同シリーズの Culpeper(1997), *History of English* など、20 世紀の後半以降、その数も増える。近年では、Johnson(2016), *The History of Early English: An Activity-based Approach* のような個性的なものもある[2]。Trask(1994), *Language Change* は、この流れの比較的早い時期のものであると言える。

これを踏まえて、注釈を付与する際には、本文中の EXERCISE に加えて、さらにワークを追加することに重点を置いた。注釈者が新たに加えたワークは、「練習問題」と表記することで *Language Change* 本体の EXERCISE と区別を行う。また、新たに追加した練習問題には、レベル分けを付した。レベル 1 が最も入門的で、応用を含むレベル 2 とレベル 3 は、その度合いに応じて段階をつけた。必要に応じて取捨選択しながら練習問題を利用して欲しい。すべての練習問題に取り組むことは、必ずしも想定されていない。

Language Change の初版は 1994 年であるので、本書の記述には、My turntable needs the stylus changed(p. 36)のような、現代の読者の生活にはなじまない例文も含まれる。このため、本書には若干の「古さ」を感じる面があるかもしれない。現代英語の最新の情報やインターネットの拡大による言語を取り巻く環境の変化についての記述も、必ずしも十分であるとは言えない。しかし、その点を考慮しても、「語彙の変化」「発音の変化」「綴り字の変化」「文法の変化」というように扱う対象をきれいに整理した

上で、必要な情報を簡潔に分かりやすく要約し、言語変化の面白さを読者に提示していく本書の記述の軽快さは魅力的である。練習問題では現代英語の近年の変化に関する問いも追加したので、これらを利用して本書が書かれたあとの 21 世紀の英語の変化を補いながら、それぞれの読者が考える言語変化の世界を構築して欲しい。

　最後に、本書に注釈を付して出版するにあたり、多くの方々のお世話になった。三重大学の西村秀夫先生と東京外国語大学の大谷直輝先生には、注釈の全文をお読みいただき、貴重なご助言をいただいた。また、本書の出版をお認めくださったひつじ書房の松本功氏、編集をご担当くださった海老澤絵莉氏には、本書の出版に至るまで、さまざまなご支援をいただいた。この場を借りて、お世話になったすべての方々に謝意を表したい。

2019 年 3 月 22 日
家入葉子

注

1　*The Guardian*（2004 年 4 月 8 日）に掲載された R. L. Trask についての記事（https://www.theguardian.com/news/2004/apr/08/guardianobituaries1）を参照。

2　この英語史については、筆者の書評も参照（家入 2019）。

CONTENTS

Acknowledgements		*vi*
Using this book		*vii*
1	Language is always changing	1
2	English in the past	7
3	Borrowing words	12
4	Creating words	19
5	Change in pronunciation	25
6	Change in spelling	31
7	Change in grammar	36
8	Change in meaning	41
9	The origin of dialects	46
10	Relatedness between languages	51
11	More remote relations	58
12	The birth and death of languages	64
13	Attitudes towards language change	72
14	Putting it all together	78
	Further reading	*81*
	Appendix	*86*
	Index	*91*

ACKNOWLEDGEMENTS

I am indebted to Dick Hudson for suggesting and encouraging this work, and to Claire L'Enfant, Joanna Legg and Emma Cotter at Routledge for their support and very considerable patience. Earlier drafts of the book were read, in part or in whole, by Dick Hudson, Richard Coates, Lisa Wale and a number of anonymous student readers; I am grateful for their comments and suggestions, and perhaps I should have taken their advice more often. Lisa Wale also kindly tracked down some elusive information for me. Berry Harper, Ann Fletcher and Sharon Groves dealt efficiently with a number of software problems that were beyond me.

For the second printing, I am indebted to William Bright and Max Wheeler for bringing to my attention a number of minor errors; these have now been corrected.

Scrabble ® is a registered trademark owned in the United States by Hasbro Inc., in Canada by Hasbro International Inc., in Australia by Murfitt Regency Pty Ltd, Victoria, and elsewhere by J.W. Spear & Sons PLC, Enfield, England.

USING THIS BOOK

As the title suggests, this is a workbook on language change. It is not a textbook, and it is not designed to present you with a vast amount of information: other books are available if you would like to read further on the topic. Instead, this one aims to help you start thinking about some of the important ideas in the study of language change. Each unit introduces one aspect of the topic with a few examples; most of the examples are taken from English at first, though, as you work through the book, you will see more and more examples from other languages.

Roughly halfway through each unit you will encounter an exercise in the form of some data relevant to that unit's topic. You should work through the exercise as carefully and thoughtfully as you can; in some cases, you are advised to discuss the exercise with your classmates. Very often a set of answers is provided for this first exercise, so that you can check you are on the right track.

At the end of each unit are several more exercises, which you should tackle in the same careful way. For these exercises, though, answers are usually not provided, or only sample answers are given. You should work through all these exercises as thoughtfully as you can, since the whole point of this workbook is to help you gain an understanding of language change by getting to grips with real data and learning to make sense of it.

At the end of the book there is a small appendix of information about some of the English words that crop up in the exercises; you may find it helpful to refer to this while attempting some of the exercises. For additional help, you may like to refer to a good dictionary of English, especially to one that provides information about the history of each word.

If you would like to read more about language change, either in general or on particular topics, a list of some suitable books is given in the **Further Reading** at the end of the workbook. Some additional exercises, in the form of projects, are also suggested there.

LANGUAGE IS ALWAYS CHANGING

> Every language that people use changes constantly. English, for example, has been changing throughout its history and it is still changing today.

How do you address a woman when you don't know if she's married or not? A man can always be safely addressed as 'Mr So-and-so', but, for most of the twentieth century, English provided only the forms 'Mrs So-and-so' for a married woman and 'Miss So-and-so' for an unmarried one. If you didn't know whether the woman you were addressing was married, you were forced into an embarrassing guess, with every chance of getting it wrong.

But things have changed. A few years ago, a new word appeared in English: *Ms*, variously pronounced 'miz' or 'muss'. Now you can safely address a woman as '*Ms* So-and-so' without committing yourself to an awkward guess. If you look in a good recent dictionary, you will find *Ms* entered there, but, if your dictionary is more than a few years old, you probably won't find it.

What conclusions can we draw? Well, one possible conclusion is that you need a new dictionary. More importantly, though, we can conclude that English has *changed* in this small respect: a few years ago this word didn't exist, but now it does.

This example is in no way unusual or remarkable: whether we are aware of it or not, English is changing all the time. New words are constantly coming into use, and not only new words, but also new pronunciations and even new grammatical forms. At the same time, old words, old forms and old pronunciations are gradually dropping out of use.

Moreover, this constant change is not some new and alarming development. English, as we shall be demonstrating, has been changing throughout its history in the same sorts of ways, and the same is true of every other living language. One of the fundamental things you need to understand about languages is that they are always changing.

This book is about language change. We shall be looking at some of the ways in which languages change, and we shall also try to understand something about why they change. After that, we shall be looking at some of the consequences of language change, and at the way people react to it when they notice it.

EXERCISE

1.0 You have probably noticed that the English spoken in North America differs in a number of obvious ways from the English spoken in Britain. North American speakers say *I've just gotten a letter*; British speakers say *I've just got a letter*. Americans get their hot water from a *faucet*; British speakers get theirs from a *tap*. The season after summer is *fall* on one side of the Atlantic, but *autumn* on the other. And many words, such as *missile* and *tomato*, are pronounced very differently. What do you think is the reason for these differences?

Please don't read any further until you have thought about this question and perhaps discussed it.

Comment

English was introduced to North America from Britain in the seventeenth century. Most famously, the Pilgrim Fathers (and Mothers) sailed from Plymouth to Massachusetts in 1620, taking English with them. What happened? Well, they certainly didn't leave Plymouth saying 'Pip pip, old chap – must toddle along', and then arrive in Massachusetts crying 'Hey, buddy – have a nice day, now' at the first native Americans they saw. They took with them the same English they had spoken in England. But, as the generations passed, English continued to change on both sides of the Atlantic, just as it had always done in Britain. Unsurprisingly, though, it didn't always change in the same way in both places. The great barrier to communication posed by the Atlantic Ocean ensured that changes taking place on one side did not always reach the other side, and so, with the passage of time, the two varieties of English gradually grew more and more different from each other. As we shall see later, the combination of language change and geographical separation can have far-reaching consequences.

And what about my particular examples? Well, *I've just gotten a letter* was the form used by almost everybody in Britain in the seventeenth century, and it's still used in North America; in Britain, however, *gotten* was later replaced by *got*. The native English word *fall* has been retained in North America; in Britain, the word *autumn*, borrowed from French, finally replaced it in the nineteenth century.

On the other hand, British English has retained the native word *tap*, while American speech eventually settled on *faucet*, another French loan word. All four of these words were actually in use in seventeenth-century Britain, but the two groups of speakers have made different choices. The seventeenth-century British pronunciation of *missile* is still used, more or less, in North America, where the word sounds just like *missal*; in Britain, though, the pronunciation of this word was drastically changed in the nineteenth century under the influence of the spelling, which reminded people of *mile*. Finally, *tomato* is a different case: the word scarcely existed in seventeenth-century English, since the plant itself was only introduced into Britain from Mexico a few years before the Pilgrims sailed, and even then it was commonly called the *love-apple* and was widely regarded as poisonous. When they eventually learned this word, British and North American speakers settled on different pronunciations for it, just as, when the motor car was invented centuries later, British speakers decided to call certain parts of it the *bonnet* and the *boot*, while North Americans decided instead to call these the *hood* and the *trunk*.

There is another factor to consider, which you may have thought of. You are doubtless aware that the English spoken in, say, Yorkshire is noticeably different from the English spoken in, say, Dorset. The same, of course, was true in the seventeenth century. Could these dialect differences have had something to do with the development of North American speech?

To a certain extent, yes. New England (the northeastern part of the United States) was largely settled by immigrants from the south of England, not from the north or from Scotland, and still today the speech of New England sounds more like southern British speech than do other North American varieties. Western Pennsylvania, in contrast, was mostly settled by the Ulster Scots (people from Ireland whose ancestors had come from Scotland). Even today, a housewife in Pittsburgh will say she is going to *redd up the house* (meaning that she's going to tidy it up); the word *redd*, meaning *tidy up*, is still used today in many parts of Scotland, but, outside Scotland and western Pennsylvania, this word is almost completely unknown to speakers of English. Nevertheless, it seems clear that such dialect differences in Britain are reflected in only very minor ways in North American speech: the differences between British English and North American English are overwhelmingly the result of changes which have occurred since the seventeenth century.

SUMMARY

- Every living language is constantly changing, in vocabulary, in pronunciation and in grammar.
- This change is natural and inevitable, and it should not be grounds for alarm or condemnation.

EXERCISES

1.1 The 1990 edition of the *Longman Register of New Words* lists over a thousand new English words recorded for the first time in 1988–90. Here are a few of them. How many of them are immediately familiar to you? How many are at least vaguely familiar? And how many totally unfamiliar?

agg	fattist
all-seater	fatwah
Balearic	geeky
basho	glass cockpit
B-boy/B-girl	Gorbymania
bimboy	jheri curl
blag	karaoke
blush (as in *Janet blushed herself*)	lager lout
	Lambada
bum bag	libero
bunt	mad cow disease
callanetics	motormouth
cardboard city	noodle western
charge-capping	rai
daytimer	scrum pox
Deep House	sicko
diffuser	skippy
dreads	skorts
dweeb	zero option
eco-friendly	zouk

1.2 When the English-speaking immigrants settled in North America, they encountered a number of plants, animals and objects which they had never seen before, and for which they had no names. Among these were skunks, raccoons, moose, chipmunks, tobacco, maize, squash (a type of vegetable), wigwams and tomahawks. Now, of course, we have English names for all of these. Where do you suppose these names came from?

1.3 It was mentioned in the text that the words *autumn* and *faucet* were borrowed from French, even though English already had the words *fall* and *tap* with the same meanings. In fact, these are just two of thousands of English words borrowed from French, a few of the others being *castle, government, country, army, beef, roast, fool, fruit, letter, horrible, gentle* and *mirror*. Can you think of any reason why English speakers should have borrowed French words so freely?

1.4 We have seen that geographical separation combined with the processes of language change leads to regional differences.

Consequently, every regional variety of English has its own distinguishing characteristics which, to a certain extent, set it apart from other varieties of English. Here are a few words which are more or less typical of each of several regional varieties. Can you recognize the variety in each case? (Of course, it is possible that one of these varieties is yours.) The first one is done for you.

Variety A: *volk* 'people', 'nation'
veld 'countryside'
mbaqanga 'style of pop music'
indaba 'conference'
robot 'traffic light'
sloot 'ditch'

You might be able to spot that the words *volk*, *veld* and *sloot* are of Dutch origin, while *mbaqanga* and *indaba* are words of African origin. The variety is South African English, which has been strongly influenced by the other major languages of South Africa, Afrikaans (a close relative of Dutch), Zulu and Xhosa (the two principal Bantu languages of the country).

Variety B: *fair dinkum* 'genuine', 'true'
bonzer 'excellent'
sheila 'woman', 'girl'
cooee 'hello'
barbie 'barbecue'
dinky-di 'typical'

Variety C: *burn* 'stream'
carry-out 'takeaway'
dreich 'dull'
shoogle 'wobble'
rone 'drainpipe'
outwith 'outside'

Variety D: *scram* 'puny'
barm 'yeast'
bide 'stay'
smeech 'smoke', 'smell'
chibboles 'spring onions'
gall 'blister'

Variety E: *duppy* 'ghost'
vex 'annoyed'
dunny 'money'
look for 'visit'
peelhead 'bald person'
ganja 'marijuana'

Variety F: *dacoit* 'bandit'
stepney 'spare wheel'
dhobi 'washerman'

tiffin 'snack'
mixy-grinder 'food blender'
crore 'ten million'

Variety G: *maven* 'expert'
zucchini 'courgettes'
broil 'grill'
washcloth 'face flannel'
barrette 'hairslide'
suspenders 'braces'

ENGLISH IN THE PAST 2

> As we look at older and older samples of English, the language becomes increasingly difficult and strange, and the earliest English is an utterly foreign language to us. In a thousand years, English has changed beyond recognition.

In the last unit I remarked that English has been changing throughout its history. Now we're going to look at some examples of English from earlier centuries, to give you an idea of how much the language has changed in the last thousand years or so. Let's begin with the opening of Shakespeare's play *As You Like It*, which was written around the year 1600. Orlando is speaking to Adam:

> As I remember, Adam, it was upon this fashion bequeathed me by will but poor a thousand crowns; and, as thou sayest, charged my brother on his blessing, to breed me well; and there begins my sadness. My brother Jacques he keeps at school, and report speaks goldenly of his profit: for my part, he keeps me rustically at home, or, to speak more properly, stays me here at home unkept; for call you that keeping for a gentleman of my birth, that differs not from the stalling of an ox?

You may already have read some of Shakespeare's plays, but, even if you have not, you can probably understand most of this with little difficulty. Nevertheless, it seems strange to us: we just don't *say* things that way.

EXERCISE

2.0 Here are a few phrases from the passage. How would you say them in modern English?

(a) upon this fashion
(b) as thou sayest
(c) charged my brother . . . to breed me well
(d) report speaks goldenly of his profit
(e) he . . . stays me here at home unkept
(f) call you that keeping?
(g) that differs not . . .

Comment

Here are some suggested modern versions; of course, you've probably come up with something a little different:

(a) '(in) this way'; 'like this'
(b) 'as you say'
(c) 'told my brother to bring me up well'
(d) 'they say he's doing very well'
(e) 'he leaves me here at home with no money'
(f) 'do you call that keeping?'
(g) 'which isn't different . . .'

Some of the phrases in the passage are stranger than others. For example, the phrase 'report speaks goldenly of his profit' certainly sounds very unnatural, but it's clearly a sentence of English. On the other hand, 'call you that keeping?' is simply impossible in modern English: can you imagine anyone asking *Call you that a good record?* Here we have an example of a change in English grammar which has occurred between Shakespeare's time and our own: modern English absolutely requires *Do you call that a good record?*, or, more informally, *Call that a good record?*

Early Modern English

Shakespeare wrote about four hundred years ago, but the English he used is still called by scholars EARLY MODERN ENGLISH. Let's now look at something a bit earlier. The English poet Geoffrey Chaucer died in 1400; the following lines are taken the Prologue to his greatest work, the *Canterbury Tales*. They were written in about 1387; the poet is apologizing for the apparent crudeness of some of the stories he is 'repeating':

But first I pray yow, of youre curteisye,
That ye narette it nat my vileynye,
Thogh that I pleynly speke in this mateere,
To telle yow hir wordes and hir cheere,
Ne thogh I speke hir wordes proprely,
For this ye knowen al so wel as I,
Who so shal telle a tale after a man,

> He moote reherce as ny as euere he kan
> Euerich a word, if it be in his charge,
> Al speke he neuer so rudeliche or large,
> Or ellis he moot telle his tale vntrewe,
> Or feyne thing, or fynde wordes newe.

Chaucer wrote about two centuries before Shakespeare, and his English is far more difficult to understand: scholars call the English of this period MIDDLE ENGLISH. Part of the problem, of course, is the strange spelling of the time (strange to us, that is). You can probably recognize *curteisye* as 'courtesy', *vileynye* as 'villainy', *reherce* as 'rehearse', *ellis* as 'else' and *vntrewe* as 'untrue', but you might have been defeated by *euerich* for 'every' and *rudelich* for 'rudely'. But, even with the spellings cleared up, you would still find great difficulty in making sense of this passage. For one thing, some of Chaucer's words have changed their meanings since he used them: when Chaucer wrote 'villainy', he meant merely 'incivility', 'lack of good breeding'; when he wrote 'cheer', he meant 'state of mind'; when he wrote 'rehearse' he meant 'repeat'. For another, some of his words have disappeared from the language: the word *arette*, for example, meant 'consider', 'reckon', and its strangely formed negative *narette*, which occurs in this passage, therefore meant 'not to consider'. This word had completely dropped out of use by about 1650.

Middle English

Another major problem, but one which is difficult to demonstrate here, is Chaucer's pronunciation. In 1400 the pronunciation of English was astonishingly different from the pronunciation of today. Just to give one example, observe that the words *mateere* 'matter' and *cheere* 'cheer', in lines 3 and 4, are rhymes for Chaucer: both of these words were pronounced differently from the way we pronounce them now. The word *cheere* was pronounced something like 'chair a' (like 'a chair' the wrong way round), and *mateere* rhymed perfectly with this.

Middle English cannot be read without special study, but we have not yet reached the earliest English spoken in Britain, from the period scholars call OLD ENGLISH. The following extract comes from the *Anglo-Saxon Chronicle*, an annual record of events kept by English monks about a thousand years ago. I have carefully selected a comparatively easy passage: good luck! (ð and þ = modern English *th*; æ = modern English *a*.)

Old English

> Brittene igland is ehta hund mila lang and twa hund brad, and her sind on þis iglande fif geþeode: Englisc and Brytwylsc and Scyttisc and Pyhtisc and Bocleden. Erest weron bugend þises landes Brittes; þa coman of Armenia and gesætan suðewearde Bryttene ærost . . .

Can you make any sense of this at all? Probably not much. Here is a translation:

> 'The island of Britain is eight hundred miles long and two hundred wide, and there are on this island five languages:

English and British–Welsh and Scottish and Pictish and Book-Latin. The first settlers of this land were the British; they came from Armenia and they settled southern Britain first . . .'

With the translation, you can probably pick out some bits and pieces of recognizable English in the passage, but mostly it remains as unfamiliar as, say, modern Dutch.

Yet this is not Dutch – it's English. This is in some sense the same language you speak every day. The people who spoke this early version of English passed it on to their children, who passed it on to *their* children, who passed it on to THEIR children, who . . . until it finally reached you. But it has reached you in a very different state. A thousand years is only about forty generations, but during those forty generations the language has been changing: a new word here, a new pronunciation there, a new grammatical form somewhere else, and – well, you see the result.

SUMMARY

- Like all languages, English has been changing throughout its history.
- In the space of about a thousand years, it has changed virtually beyond recognition.
- Earlier forms of English are now so unfamiliar to us that we cannot read them without special study.

EXERCISES

2.1 Here are some further quotations from Shakespeare's plays. What differences can you observe between Shakespeare's English and our own?

(a) Our remedies oft in ourselves do lie
Which we ascribe to heaven.
(b) How now, wit! Whither wander you?
(c) Hath not old custom made this life more sweet
Than that of painted pomp?
(d) A bloody deed! almost as bad, good mother,
As kill a king and marry with his brother.
(e) All is not well; I doubt some foul play.
(f) But, soft! Methinks I scent the morning air.
(g) What do you read, my lord?
[addressed to Hamlet, who is reading a book]
(h) The frame and huge foundation of the earth
Shak'd like a coward.
(i) This was the most unkindest cut of all.
(j) 'Tis a naughty night to swim in.

2.2 Certain English words have a decidedly strange spelling, with 'silent' letters included. Here are a few examples:

write, wrong, wrestle, wring (silent *w*)
night, light, bright, sight (silent *gh*)
knot, knit, knife, knee (silent *k*)
castle, fasten, listen, rustle (silent *t*)
lamb, comb, tomb, bomb (silent *b*)
walk, folk, should, talk (silent *l*)
take, ride, give, name (silent *e*)

What do you suppose is the reason for this?

2.3 Using the appendix provided at the end of this book where necessary, try to translate into modern English the passage from Chaucer given in the text.

2.4 The following extract is taken from the Paston letters, the voluminous correspondence of the Paston family of Norfolk; it dates from 1476, just about the time that scholars consider that Middle English was giving way to Modern English. Using, where necessary, the appendix provided at the end of this book, translate it into modern English as best you can, and comment on any characteristics of its language that strike you. John Paston is writing to Margery Brews; the text has been modernized here in a few respects, and all of the numerous abbreviations of the original have been spelled out in full.

> Mastresse, thow so be that I, vnaqweyntyd wyth yow as yet, tak vp on me to be thus bold as to wryght on to yow wyth ought your knowlage and leve, yet, mastress, for syche pore seruyse as I now in my mind owe yow, purposyng, ye not dyspleasyd, duryng my lyff to contenu the same, I beseche yow to pardon my boldness, and not to dysdeyn, but to accepte thys sympyll bylle to recomand me to yow in syche wyse as I best can or may jmagyn to your most plesure. And, mastress, for svch report as I haue herd of yow by many and dyuerse persones, and specyally by my ryght trusty frend, Rychard Stratton, berer her of, to whom I beseche yow to geue credence in syche maters as he shall on my behalue comon wyth yow of, if it lyhe yow to lystyn hym. . . . Her I send yow thys bylle wretyn wyth my lewd hand and sealyd wyth my sygnet to remayn wyth yow for a wyttnesse ayenste me, and to my shame and dyshonour if I contrary it.

3 BORROWING WORDS

> Speakers of a language may 'borrow' (that is, copy) words from other languages which they have encountered. English has borrowed many thousands of words from other languages, and is still doing so today.

One of the most obvious kinds of change in language is the appearance of new words. This kind of change can be quite conspicuous: you may actually notice the first time you encounter a new word (though, as we shall see later, you may not). New words have been pouring into English at a prodigious rate throughout its history, and the rate of appearance of new words is now perhaps greater than at any previous period. One of the major tasks faced by lexicographers (dictionary writers) in preparing their new editions is to collect the thousands of new words which have appeared since their last editions. Some publishers even bring out an annual volume of new words. Where do all these new words come from?

As we saw in **Unit 1**, one very obvious source of new words is foreign languages. There are several reasons why English speakers (or others) might want to take over a foreign word. The simplest one is that the word is the name for something new. When the English settlers in North America encountered an animal they'd never seen before, with a masked face and a ringed tail, they naturally asked the local Indians what *they* called it. What the Indians said sounded to the English speakers like 'raccoon', and that therefore became the English name for this beautiful creature. Similarly, when the English discovered that the Gaelic speakers of the Scottish Highlands were producing a most agreeable beverage, they asked what it was called. The Scots replied with their Gaelic name for it, *uisgebeatha*, which means 'water of life' in Gaelic. This name was taken into English as *whiskybae* and quickly shortened to *whisky*.

This particular word, by the way, has continued to travel. As the knowledge of whisky has spread across Europe and the world, its Gaelic name has travelled with it. In most European languages, the word *whisky* has been taken over as the name of the beverage. Even in faraway Japan, whisky is now consumed and is known in Japanese as *uisukii*.

The name of another familiar beverage has made a similar journey. Many centuries ago, the people of Ethiopia discovered that a delicious hot beverage could be made from the beans of a bush which grew locally. They passed on the beverage, and their name for it, to the neighbours the Arabs. The Arabs in turn passed both on to the Turks, who became famous for their skill at preparing the beverage. The Turks then introduced both the drink and the name to the Europeans, and particularly to the Italians, who also became famous for their distinctive way of preparing the stuff. English visitors to Italy returned home full of enthusiasm for the new beverage, and the ancient Ethiopian name finally passed into English in the form *coffee*.

EXERCISE

3.0 The practice of taking a word from one language into another is somewhat curiously known as BORROWING. Below is a list of English words all of which were originally borrowed from foreign languages as the name of objects or customs which were themselves borrowed from speakers of other languages. See if you can guess in each case which language is the source of the word. Some are quite easy, while others are rather difficult.

(a) kayak
(b) cafeteria
(c) soprano
(d) tulip
(e) coach
(f) kangaroo
(g) ballet
(h) tea
(i) palaver
(j) democracy
(k) khaki
(l) tsunami
(m) mayonnaise
(n) yacht
(o) sex
(p) waltz
(q) ukulele
(r) sauna
(s) denim
(t) ski
(u) juggernaut
(v) algebra

Answers and comments

(a) *kayak*: from Eskimo. The Eskimos, of course, invented the kayak.
(b) *cafeteria*: from Spanish. The word means simply 'coffee shop' in Spanish, but in English we have applied it to something rather different.
(c) *soprano*: from Italian. Italian has long been known as the language of music, and English has borrowed dozens of musical terms from Italian.
(d) *tulip*: from Turkish (no, not from Dutch!). The name is derived from the Turkish word for 'turban', since the

flower resembles a medieval Turkish turban.
(e) *coach*: from Hungarian. The first coaches were built in Hungary, and named after the Hungarian town of Kocs (pronounced 'coach').
(f) *kangaroo*: from an unidentified Australian language. Over 200 languages were spoken in Australia before the Europeans arrived, but most are now extinct or close to extinction.
(g) *ballet*: from French. French was long known as the language of high culture, and many English words in the domain of art and literature come from French.
(h) *tea*: from Chinese. The Chinese were the first to drink tea, and two of their words for it, *te* and *cha*, have been borrowed throughout the world.
(i) *palaver*: from Portuguese. The Portuguese original means simply 'talk'.
(j) *democracy*: from Greek. The Greeks, of course, invented democracy, and the Greek word means literally 'government by the people'.
(k) *khaki*: from Urdu (a major language of Pakistan). The word comes ultimately from Persian, where it means 'dusty'.
(l) *tsunami*: from Japanese. Tsunamis (tidal waves) are a constant worry in the volcanically active and earthquake-prone islands on the rim of the Pacific.
(m) *mayonnaise*: from French. The great prestige of French cuisine has brought many French culinary terms into English.
(n) *yacht*: from Dutch. The Dutch have long been noted seamen, and many English nautical terms derive from Dutch.
(o) *sex*: from Latin. The word is derived from the Latin verb meaning 'to divide': the human race is 'divided' into two sexes. The words 'section' and 'sector' come from the same Latin root.
(p) *waltz*: from German. The dance originated in German-speaking Vienna.
(q) *ukulele*: from Hawaiian. The Hawaiians invented the instrument, whose name curiously means 'jumping flea' in Hawaiian.
(r) *sauna*: from Finnish. The Finns have given the world both the custom and their name for it.
(s) *denim*: from French. The origin of the word is the French *de Nîmes* '(fabric) of Nîmes' (Nîmes is a city in France).
(t) *ski*: from Norwegian. Skis were, of course, invented by the Scandinavians.
(u) *juggernaut*: from Hindi. In India, a juggernaut is a huge wheeled chariot used in Hindu festivals.
(v) *algebra*: from Arabic. The medieval Arabs were distinguished mathematicians.

But encountering something new is not the only possible reason for borrowing a word from a foreign language. We saw on pages 2–3 that English speakers borrowed the words *faucet* and *autumn* from French, even though English already had the words *tap* and *fall* with the same meanings. The reason for this was prestige: for a long time, French was a more prestigious language than English, and English speakers were often eager to show off their command of this prestigious language. Such speakers are still with us today. You may actually know someone who is fond of punctuating his or her English speech with French words and phrases like *merci, au contraire, force majeure, à la mode* and *genre*. Very many French words have entered English in just this way. Even the familiar word *face* was borrowed from French into English, where it rapidly displaced the native word *anleth*, with the same meaning.

Today, however, the shoe is on the other foot. English has become the most prestigious language on earth, and speakers of Spanish, Italian, German, Japanese and even French eagerly borrow English words and phrases into their own languages. Look at any popular magazine from western Europe or even from Japan, and you will see bits of English scattered about the pages. I've just picked up an Italian magazine at random; on almost every page someone is described as a *rockstar*, a *top model*, a *sex-symbol*, a *superstar* or a *top manager*. An ad for a computer promises a *hard disk*, a *mouse* and a *floppy*. One film is labelled a *horror*, while another has a *happy-end*. Fashion articles talk about the *look* and explain what's currently *in*. And the pages are spattered with English words like *jogging, fan, gadget, hobby, T-shirt, massage parlour, zoom, pay-tv, show, home video, mass media, status* and *check-up*.

This fondness for English words has particularly upset the linguistic conservatives in France, where the authorities are constantly making efforts to stamp out the use of English borrowings. At intervals, the French government issues lists of English words which people are forbidden to use, with matching lists of 'genuine' French words which they are supposed to use instead. Government employees, including teachers, are actually obliged to follow these guidelines, but, of course, most people in France ignore them and go on using any English words that take their fancy. French speakers happily spend *le weekend* indulging in *le camping*; they often listen to *le compact-disc* or *le walkman*, and they may have a taste for *le rock* or *le jazz* or *le blues* or even *le heavy metal*. If they fancy an evening out, they may go to *le pub* to have *un scotch* or *un gin* or *un cocktail*, or they may go to see *un western* or *un strip-tease*; if not, they may stay home to read *un best-seller* or just to watch *le football* on television. It seems we are now paying back the French with interest for all the words we've borrowed from them over the years.

SUMMARY

- Languages often borrow words from other languages.
- Borrowing may take place in order to obtain words for genuinely new things, or merely for reasons of prestige.

EXERCISES

3.1 No language has borrowed English words more enthusiastically than Japanese. But the sound system of Japanese is very different from that of English (for example, Japanese has no l sound), and so borrowed English words have to be adapted to make them pronounceable in Japanese. Below is a list of Japanese words borrowed from English; see if you can recognize them. Note that the Japanese vowels *a e i o u* are pronounced roughly as in *far*, *fete*, *machine*, *post* and *rude*. I have marked the syllables which are accented in English; the vowels *u* and *i* are pronounced very weakly when short and unaccented. A few examples: *'jampaa* is 'jumper'; *'waffuru* is 'waffle'; *'miruku* is 'milk'; *appuru 'pai* is 'apple pie'.

(a) aisu ku'riimu (b) pu'rezento
(c) to'rakku (d) 'firumu
(e) kom'pyuutaa (f) bu'rondo
(g) 'gaarufurendo (h) 'serori
(i) u'etto suutsu (j) 'hambaagaa
(k) zuumu 'renzu (l) yuu-'taan
(m) 'nambaa pureeto (n) su'kaafu
(o) masu'kara (p) 'teeburu
(q) 'tii-shatsu (r) 'ai-rainaa
(s) 'basuketto booru (t) do'raiyaa
(u) 'saamosutatto (v) 'shiito beruto
(w) 'eya-hosutesu (x) e'rochikku
(y) 'herikoputaa (z) gu'reepufuruutsu

3.2 English has adopted a possibly surprising way of obtaining new scientific and technical terms. What we do is to borrow words from Latin and Ancient Greek and then combine them into new English words. For example, the word *telephone* was constructed by combining the Greek words *tele* 'far' and *phone* 'voice' into a single English word. (The ancient Greeks, of course, had no such word as *telephone*, since the device was unknown to them.) Using the appendix at the end of this book where necessary, identify the literal meanings of the Latin and Greek elements in the following English words:

(a) microphone (b) television
(c) multilingual (d) polyglot
(e) thermometer (f) pseudoscience
(g) ultrasonic (h) transvestite
(i) atmosphere (j) hydrodynamics

(k) psychology   (l) bibliophile
(m) hypodermic   (n) viticulture
(o) dinosaur   (p) rhododendron
(q) amphibian   (r) vivisection
(s) helicopter   (t) submarine

3.3 Sometimes it is easy to tell, from its distinctive form, that an English word has been borrowed from another language. You will hardly be surprised to learn that *geisha* and *judo* come from Japanese, that *aria* and *fresco* come from Italian, or that *schmuck* and *shtumm* come from Yiddish. But there is one large group of borrowed words in English which is far more difficult to recognize, since the words in question are all but indistinguishable from native English words. Among these words are the following:

fellow	kilt	scowl	skirt
gear	kindle	scrape	sky
get	law	scrub	take
give	rag	sister	they
hit	scatter	skill	want
kick	score	skin	window

These words were largely borrowed during the tenth and eleventh centuries. What language do you suppose they come from? (Hint: the British place names *Grimsby*, *Derby*, *Whitby*, *Crosby*, *Scunthorpe* and *Lowestoft* (among many others) come from the same source.)

3.4 Unsurprisingly, many English names for items of food and drink are borrowed from a wide variety of other languages. Here are a few such English words, with a list of the languages from which these words are *ultimately* derived (some of them came into English via several intermediary languages); can you match them up? (For example, (1) matches with (k); you may be aware that potatoes and maize, among other food crops, were introduced to Europe from the New World.)

(1) potato, maize, persimmon, cashew (a) Japanese
(2) curry, mango   (b) Nahuatl (Aztec)
(3) caviar, yogurt, doner (kebab)   (c) Dutch
(4) asparagus, pepper, butter, parsley (d) Spanish
(5) punch, samosa, chutney   (e) German
(6) wine, cheese, lettuce, cucumber, radish
                                      (f) Russian
(7) ketchup, lychee, kumquat   (g) Modern Greek
(8) okra, yam, banana   (h) Arabic
(9) marzipan, semolina, celery, macaroni
                                      (i) Medieval French
(10) brandy, pickle, coleslaw   (j) Portuguese

18 BORROWING WORDS

(11) veal, vinegar, cabbage, mustard
(12) sukiyaki, soy (sauce)
(13) muesli, noodle, frankfurter, pretzel
(14) avocado, chocolate, chilli, cocoa
(15) saffron, kebab, lemon, sorbet
(16) borsht, vodka
(17) caramel, vanilla, gazpacho, sherry
(18) moussaka, retsina
(19) cinnamon, cumin
(20) gateau, champagne, mousse, ragout
(21) goulash, paprika, pastrami
(22) orange, spinach
(23) port, marmalade, coco(nut), molasses

(k) American languages
(l) Hungarian/Rumanian
(m) Modern French
(n) Hindi
(o) Italian
(p) Ancient Greek
(q) Tamil
(r) African languages
(s) Persian
(t) Turkish
(u) Latin
(v) Chinese
(w) Hebrew and related languages

CREATING WORDS

4

> English, like other languages, has a wide variety of devices for creating new words from its existing resources, including compounding, prefixation and suffixation, as well as more unusual devices.

While borrowing words from other languages is a very obvious source of new words, it is very far from being the only one. There are many different ways in which the speakers of a language can coin new words by using only the existing resources of their language. In this unit we shall be looking at some of these.

In English and in many other languages, a common device for obtaining new words is COMPOUNDING – that is, combining two existing words into a single new word. From its earliest days, English has made frequent use of this device. Familiar examples include *blackboard, girlfriend, gingerbread, overhead, daredevil, mainland, paperback, sidestep, scarecrow, strip-tease, rattlesnake, hatchback* and *skinhead*. Occasionally a new word is derived by combining two existing words with a suffix, as in *blue-eyed, bookkeeper, sky diving* and *plastic-coated*. Some of these compounds have been in the language for centuries, while others are of very recent formation. Among the most recently formed English compounds are *ozone-friendly, overborrowed, laptop* and *high-five*.

Compounding

✐ **EXERCISE**

4.0 Many of the earliest English compounds to be created have since been replaced by other words and have disappeared from the language. Here are a few of these, with literal translations. What do you suppose is the modern English word with the same meaning? (æ = modern English *a*; ð = modern English *th*.)

(a) *boc-cræftig* 'book-crafty'
(b) *heah-fæder* 'high-father'
(c) *leorning-cniht* 'learning-boy'
(d) *heah-burg* 'high-city'
(e) *god-spellere* 'good-newser'
(f) *to-cuman* 'to-come'
(g) *wið-sprecan* 'against-speak'
(h) *tungol-witega* 'star-sage'

Answers and comments

(a) 'learned', 'erudite'
(b) 'patriarch'
(c) 'disciple', 'apprentice'
(d) 'capital'
(e) 'evangelist'
(f) 'arrive'
(g) 'contradict'
(h) 'astrologer'

The modern words which have replaced these ancient English compounds are nearly all borrowed or derived from French, Latin or Greek. If English had not come so powerfully under the influence of these foreign languages, many of these ancient compounds might have survived to the present day, and modern English might have a very different look to it.

Derivation

Another important way of obtaining new words is by DERIVATION – that is, by adding prefixes and suffixes to existing words. Like nearly all languages, English has extensive derivational resources. Consider, for example, the common suffix *-al*, which usually forms adjectives from nouns. Here are just a few of the noun–adjective pairs related by this suffix (some of these were not formed within English):

culture	cultural
person	personal
profession	professional
season	seasonal
statistic	statistical
ancestor	ancestral
dialect	dialectal
ornament	ornamental
triumph	triumphal
agriculture	agricultural
medicine	medicinal
origin	original
residue	residual

The suffix *-al* is just one of dozens of important derivational suffixes in English. A few of the others are *-ness* (as in *happiness*), *-ful* (as in *powerful*), *-ous* (as in *mountainous*), *-less* (as in *topless*) and *-ic* (as in *economic*). Multiple suffixation is possible: *economy/economic/economical*; *hope/hopeless/hopelessness*.

Prefixes are hardly less important in English. Among English words formed with the aid of prefixes are *trans-Atlantic, archenemy, underfunding, malformed, micro-organism, subhuman, vice-president, stepmother, demigod, counterbalance, unfamiliar, inhospitable, miniskirt, megastar, pseudoscience* and *ultraliberal*. Multiple prefixes occur, as in *polyunsaturated* and *undischarged*.

Prefixes and suffixes may be combined in deriving new words: *pre-industrial, non-magnetic, antiperspirant, uncooperative, overgeneralization*.

Affixes which were previously little used may suddenly become highly productive. This has happened with the ancient English suffix *-wise*, formerly confined to a handful of items like *clockwise, lengthwise, otherwise* and *likewise*. Within the last few years, this suffix has suddenly become enormously popular, and new coinages like *moneywise, healthwise, profitwise* and *fitnesswise* have proliferated. A similar case is that of the prefix *mega-*, once confined to technical terms like *megawatt* and *megaphone*; now it turns up routinely in formations like *megastar, megahit* and *megacity*.

Even more spectacular is the case of the prefix *mini-*. This did not even exist before the 1960s, and its first use was apparently in the new word *miniskirt*. Since then, this newly created prefix has achieved staggering popularity: new words like *mini-war, mini-budget, mini-novel* and *minibus* are almost threatening to drive the word *small* out of the language.

Less frequent than derivation, but increasingly important in English word formation, is the opposite process of BACK-FORMATION. **Back-formation** Back-formation may be losely defined as the removal from a word of something that is *apparently* (but not actually) an affix. To see how this works, consider first the familiar derivational process whereby the agent suffix *-er* derives a noun from a verb: *write* → *writer*; *sing* → singer; *smoke* → *smoker*; and so on. Now English has long had a number of nouns denoting various types of profession which happen to end in a syllable that sounds like *-er*, such as *editor, pedlar, sculptor, burglar* and *lecher*. Since these words *sound* like *writer, singer* and *smoker*, English speakers have, at various times, 'removed' the apparent suffix and hence created, by back-formation, the new verbs *edit, peddle, sculpt, burgle* and *le(t)ch*.

Slightly more subtle instances of back-formation are the verbs *baby-sit* and *sky-dive*, created from the earlier nouns *baby-sitter* and *sky-diving*. The word *baby-sitter* is actually a compound of *baby* and *sitter*, but it has been reanalysed as though it consisted of the verb *baby-sit* and the agent suffix *-er*; much the same is true of the other example.

Rather more drastic than back-formation is the process of CLIPPING, in which a word is created by extracting an arbitrary **Clipping** portion of a longer word of identical meaning. Examples of words created in this way are *phone* (from *telephone*), *bus* (from *omnibus*), *zoo* (from *zoological garden*), *gym* (from *gymnasium*), *fridge* (from *refrigerator*), *porn* (from *pornography*), *deli* (from *delicatessen*), *mimeo* (from *mimeograph*), *mike* (from *microphone*), *veg* (from *vegetable*), *shrink* (from *head-shrinker* 'psychoanalyst'), *sitcom* (from *situation comedy*), *bra* (from *brassiere*), *fax* (from *facsimile transmission*), *polythene* (from *polyethylene)* and the American *auto* (from *automobile)* and *ump* (from *umpire*). Sometimes a diminutive suffix is added during the creation of the clipped form, as in *veggie* (from *vegetarian*) and the Australian *umpy* (from *umpire*). Note, by the way, that such formations are true words; they are *not* 'abbreviations'.

Blending

Even more spectacular than clipping is the process of BLENDING, in which arbitrary portions of two words are chopped off and stitched together to form a new word. This process began in a small way several decades ago, with the coining of words like *smog* (from *smoke + fog*) and *motel* (from *motor + hotel*). Recently it has become considerably more frequent, and we now have *guesstimate* (*guess + estimate*), *skyjack* (*sky + hijack*), *stagflation* (*stagnation + inflation*), *pulsar* (*pulse + quasar*), *glasphalt* (*glass + asphalt*), *chunnel* (*channel + tunnel*) and *vegeburger* (*vegetarian + hamburger*), among many others.

Acronym

Something of an extreme in such reduction processes is represented by the creation of ACRONYMS, in which a word is derived from the initial letters of a whole phrase. Examples of this include *radar* (from *RAdio Detection And Ranging*), *laser* (from *Light Amplification by the Stimulated Emission of Radiation*), *NATO* (from *North Atlantic Treaty Organization*), *WASP* (from *White Anglo-Saxon Protestant*) and *AIDS* (from *Acquired Immune Deficiency Syndrome*). Nowadays the coining of acronyms is practically an industry: no new organization can be named, no new technical term can be created, unless an appealing acronym is instantly available. Hence we have the computer language *BASIC* (from *Beginners' All-purpose Symbolic Instruction Code*, a name laboriously constructed to provide the required acronym), *ASH* (*Action on Smoking and Health*), *ASLEF* (*Associated Society of Locomotive Engineers and Firemen*) and *ORACLE* (*Optional Reception of Announcements by Coded Line Electronics*), among very many others.

SUMMARY

- A language may create new words by using its own resources.
- Among the most important ways of coining new words are compounding (combining existing words) and derivation (adding prefixes and suffixes), but many others exist.

4.1 The words in each of the following groups share a particular sort of origin, some of which have been discussed in the text and some not. See if you can identify the manner in which the words in each group were created. Sources for a few of them are provided in the appendix to this book; a good dictionary will provide sources for all of them.

(a) cardigan, sandwich, silhouette, diesel, leotard, quisling, lynch, boycott, maverick, zeppelin.
(b) jodhpurs, magenta, ascot, spa, duffel (bag), blarney, bourbon, limerick, cheddar, cologne, champagne, china.
(c) highbrow, proofread, gentleman, bloodthirsty, daredevil, homesick, redhead, air-conditioning.
(d) Lilliputian, Shangri-La, Frankenstein, man Friday, yahoo, scrooge, malapropism.
(e) slave, vandal, arabesque, frank, gothic, gyp, cravat, hooch, swede.
(f) flu, copter, gator, cello, chimp, ad, lab, piano, maths.
(g) bewitch, enslave, archenemy, stepmother, recycle, midday, misfit, demigod.

4.2 Consider the items in italic in the following examples and explain how they are formed. Can you find any further examples of English items formed in the same way?

(a) She *made up* her face.
(b) I *get up* at 7.30.
(c) She *took off* her dress.
(d) We have *run out* of milk.
(e) He's been forced to *drop out* of the race.
(f) Something has *come up*.
(g) The policeman *took down* the details.
(h) She's *making out* very well.
(i) John and Mary have *fallen out*.
(j) I'm *running in* my new car.
(k) The milk has *gone off*.

4.3 Sports and games have contributed many words and phrases to everyday English. Can you identify the sources of the expressions in the following examples?

(a) He hit me for six.
(b) Foreign languages are her strong suit.
(c) I couldn't get to first base.
(d) The first day of the sale was a real scrum.
(e) He threw in the towel.

(f) I'm going to call his bluff.
(g) He was thrown for a loss.
(h) I found myself stymied.
(i) He was pipped at the post.
(j) She came up with a splendid riposte.
(k) We held them in check.
(l) He found himself behind the eight-ball.
(m) The ball is in your court.

4.4. We saw in the last unit that English has borrowed thousands of words from other languages, particularly from French and Latin after the Norman conquest of England. Some people have occasionally objected to this massive borrowing, arguing that English would be better served by relying on its native resources for coining words instead of borrowing. In 1966 the humorist Paul Jennings offered in *Punch* an example of what English might have been like if William the Conqueror had been defeated at Hastings. Here are some extracts from Jennings' article. Do you agree that a 'pure' native English would be an improvement? (The more difficult words are explained in the appendix at the end of this book.)

> In a foregoing piece (a week ago in this same mirthboke) I wrote anent the ninehundredth yearday of the Clash of Hastings; of how in that mighty tussle, which othered our lore for coming hundredyears, indeed for all the following aftertide till Domesday, the would-be ingangers from France were smitten hip and thigh; and of how, not least, our tongue remained selfthrough and strong, unbecluttered and unbedizened with outlandish Latin-born words of French outshoot. . . . The craft and insight of our Anglish tongue for the more cunning switchmeangroups, for unthingsome and overthingsome withtakings, gives a matchless tool to bards, deepthinkers and trypiecemen. . . . If Angland had gone the way of the Betweensea Eyots there is every likelihood that our lot would have fallen forever in the Middlesea ringpath.

CHANGE IN PRONUNCIATION

5

> Like other aspects of language, pronunciation changes over time. Such change is largely responsible for the existence of different 'accents' – that is, different ways of pronouncing a language.

You will certainly have observed that different speakers of English, particularly speakers from different places, speak the language differently in other respects than in merely having some different words. Perhaps the most conspicuous difference lies in pronunciation: we say that people who pronounce English differently have different ACCENTS.   **Accent**

Let us first clarify this term a little. The word *accent*, as it is used in linguistics, simply means a particular way of pronouncing the language. Hence, *every* speaker of English has an accent. It is not just the Glasgow bricklayer, the Dorset farmer or the Jamaican pop singer who has an accent: I have an accent, you have an accent, the starchiest television newsreader has an accent, the Queen herself has an accent. Of course, you will certainly regard some accents as more familiar, or as more prestigious, than others, but this cannot change the fact that every speaker necessarily has an accent.

And the range of accents in English is fairly impressive. Even if you're not familiar with the places themselves, you are unlikely to have much difficulty in distinguishing the accent of New Orleans from that of New York, or in distinguishing the accents of Liverpool and Newcastle, or of Bristol and Brighton, or of Dublin and Belfast. Why should this be so? Why should there be so many different ways of pronouncing English?

Once again, the explanation lies principally in linguistic change across time. Over the centuries, the pronunciation of English has changed at least as much as any other aspect of the language, and, of course, it has changed in different ways in different places. In this unit, we shall consider just a few examples.

(Non-)rhotic

Consider the words *farther* and *father*. Do you pronounce these words identically or differently? And what about the words *lore* and *law*? Or *iron* and *ion*? If you pronounce these pairs identically, you have what linguists call a NON-RHOTIC accent. If you pronounce them differently, you probably have a RHOTIC accent. These terms reflect the observation that rhotic speakers actually pronounce an R-sound in the first word of each pair, though not in the second; non-rhotic speakers do not pronounce an R-sound in any of these words.

Broadly speaking, non-rhotic pronunciations are typical of the southeast of England, of the Midlands, of Wales and of much of northern England; they are also typical of Australia, New Zealand, South Africa and the east coast and the south of the United States. Rhotic accents, in contrast, are usual in the southwest of England, in Scotland and parts of northern England, in Ireland and in most of the United States and Canada.

The historical reason for this complex distribution is not hard to identify. Several centuries ago, all speakers of English used a rhotic pronunciation, distinguishing such words as *farther* and *father*, as the spelling suggests. This type of pronunciation was therefore carried to North America, which was settled in the seventeenth century. In the eighteenth century, however, the new, non-rhotic style of pronunciation appeared in the southeast of England and became fashionable; this new pronunciation began to spread over England and Wales. The West Country, Scotland and Ireland, for whatever reason, declined to accept the new fashion and continued to use their traditional rhotic speech. Australia, New Zealand and South Africa were largely settled in the nineteenth century by immigrants from England, who took with them the new non-rhotic style. Non-rhotic speech was also carried across the Atlantic to the coastal cities of the United States, which were in fairly close contact with the mother country, but the new fashion failed to cross the Appalachian Mountains, and most of the mainland of North America retained its rhotic style.

This example provides an excellent illustration of the way in which language change typically proceeds. An innovation appears in one spot and may be taken up by other speakers; if still others find the new form appealing, it may spread across a wide area of the speech community. Eventually the innovation may drive out the older form altogether, or, as in this case, it may come to a halt after establishing itself in only part of the total community, leaving the rest unaffected.

And this is not necessarily the end of the story. In England, non-rhotic speech is now generally regarded as more prestigious than rhotic, and speakers with rhotic accents from, say, the West Country sometimes strive to replace their native rhotic pronunciation with the 'posher' non-rhotic style; it is likely therefore that the non-rhotic type of pronunciation may continue to gain ground in England. In the United States, however, the situation is reversed: there rhotic pronunciation is generally regarded as more prestigious, and native speakers of non-rhotic varieties from, say, New York City will strive equally hard to acquire a rhotic accent.

CHANGE IN PRONUNCIATION 27

EXERCISE

5.0 The words in each of the following pairs are pronounced differently by some speakers of English but identically by others. Check them to see which ones you distinguish and which ones you don't. Note that there are no 'right' or 'wrong' answers here; the answers you give will simply reflect your personal accent, which will very likely be typical of the region you come from.

(a) *pore* and *paw*
(b) *pool* and *pull*
(c) *pour* and *poor*
(d) *horse* and *hoarse*
(e) *marry* and *merry*
(f) *book* and *buck*
(g) *do* and *dew*
(h) *toe* and *tow*
(i) *tyre* and *tower*
(j) *cot* and *caught*
(k) *stir* and *stare*
(l) *whine* and *wine*
(m) *threw* and *through*

Discussion

(Note that the comments about regional distribution are very rough and broad; you will not necessarily have the type of pronunciation described as typical of your region.)

(a) *Pore* and *paw* are pronounced differently by rhotic speakers but identically by most non-rhotic speakers, as discussed above.
(b) *Pool* and *pull* are pronounced identically by most speakers in Scotland but differently by almost everyone else.
(c) *Pour* and *poor* are pronounced identically by most (not all) speakers in England but differently by most (not all) American and Scottish speakers.
(d) *Horse* and *hoarse* are pronounced differently by most speakers in Scotland and Ireland and by many Americans; most others pronounce them identically.
(e) *Marry* and *merry* (and also *Mary*) are pronounced identically in most of the United States (though not on the east coast); elsewhere they are different.
(f) *Put* and *putt* are pronounced identically by many speakers in the north of England; elsewhere they are distinguished.
(g) *Do* and *dew* are identical for most Americans, for many Canadians and for some speakers in eastern England; elsewhere they are different.
(h) *Toe* and *tow* are different for some speakers in East Anglia; all other speakers pronounce them identically.
(i) *Tyre* and *tower* are pronounced identically by many people

Received pronunciation

in England who have the sort of 'posh' accent called RECEIVED PRONUNCIATION (RP), both of them often sounding like *tar*; other speakers distinguish them.

(j) *Cot* and *caught* are pronounced identically by most Canadians, by many Scots and by some Americans; other speakers distinguish them.

(k) *Stir* and *stare* are pronounced identically in many parts of northern England, including Merseyside and much of Greater Manchester, and also in Dublin; elsewhere they are distinct.

(l) *Whine* and *wine* are distinguished by nearly all Irish and Scottish speakers, and by many speakers in the USA, Canada and New Zealand; elsewhere they are pronounced identically by most speakers.

(m) *Threw* and *through* are pronounced differently by most speakers in Wales and by a few speakers in England and the United States; most others pronounce them identically.

In all but one of the above cases, the words in question were formerly pronounced differently by all speakers of English, but have fallen together in some accents. The exception is the pair *put/putt*: these words were once pronounced identically by everybody, but now only the north of England retains the older type of pronunciation, and all other accents have created a new difference.

SUMMARY

- An accent is merely a way of pronouncing a language, and hence every speaker has an accent.
- There are many different accents of English, and almost every speaker has an accent that indicates something about where he or she comes from.
- These accents mostly derive from changes in pronunciation which have affected some areas but not others.

EXERCISES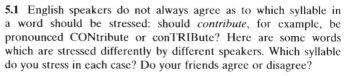

5.1 English speakers do not always agree as to which syllable in a word should be stressed: should *contribute*, for example, be pronounced CONtribute or conTRIBute? Here are some words which are stressed differently by different speakers. Which syllable do you stress in each case? Do your friends agree or disagree?

(a) adversary
(b) applicable
(c) centrifugal
(d) cigarette
(e) comparable
(f) contribute
(g) controversy
(h) (an industrial) dispute
(i) distribute
(j) exquisite
(k) ice cream
(l) kilometre
(m) magazine
(n) pejorative
(o) primarily
(p) subsidence

5.2 There is one English sound which has no traditional spelling of its own. It occurs in the middle of the English words *measure, treasure, vision, azure* and *seizure*. Many (not all) speakers also have it at the end of the words *beige, rouge* and *camouflage*; some speakers also have it at the beginning of the words *gigolo* and (*Dr*) *Zhivago*. It is the rarest of all the English consonant sounds. By considering these examples, can you work out how we acquired this sound and why we have no particular spelling for it?

5.3 Each of the English vowel letters *a, e, i, o* and *u* represents at least two quite different sounds, traditionally called the LONG and the SHORT SOUND. For example, the long and short values of *a* occur in *hate* and *hat*, respectively, the long and short values of *e* in *we* and *wet*, and the long and short values of *i* in *fine* and *fin*. Now consider the pronunciation of the following pairs of words; in each case the first word shows the 'long' pronunciation of the vowel and the second the 'short':

Long/short sounds

s*a*ne	s*a*nity
v*a*in	v*a*nity
Sp*a*in	Sp*a*niard
hum*a*ne	hum*a*nity
ser*e*ne	ser*e*nity
cl*e*an	cl*e*anliness
sal*i*ne	sal*i*nity
mal*i*gn	mal*i*gnant
cr*i*me	cr*i*minal
s*i*gn	s*i*gnify
div*i*ne	div*i*nity
m*o*de	m*o*dify
verb*o*se	verb*o*sity
c*o*ne	c*o*nical

Can you draw any conclusions about the history of the 'long' and 'short' pronunciations? (Hint: why do you suppose English speakers decided to use the same letter for the long and short vowels?)

5.4 Here are some English words which are pronounced differently by different speakers; the differing pronunciations which are in use are briefly described. Check your own pronunciations and then compare them with those of your friends to see how they match up. (Once again, there are no 'right' or 'wrong' answers here; all the pronunciations given are in good usage.)

apartheid	last syllable like 'height' or 'hate'?
apparatus	third syllable rhymes with 'mart', 'mate' or 'mat'?

ate	rhymes with 'met' or with 'mate'?
centenary	second syllable like 'ten' or like 'teen'?
deity	first syllable rhymes with 'say' or 'see'?
derisive	second syllable like 'rice' or like 'rise'?
dilemma	first syllable like 'did' or like 'die'?
economics	first syllable like 'peek' or like 'peck'?
envelope	first syllable like 'den' or like 'don'?
homosexual	first syllable like 'hot' or like 'home'?
longitude	*ng* as in 'finger' or as in 'range'?
medicine	two syllables or three?
migraine	first syllable like 'me' or like 'my'?
plastic	first syllable like 'cat' or like 'car'?
police	one syllable or two?
privacy	first syllable like 'sit' or like 'site'?
sheikh	rhymes with 'leek' or with 'lake'?
status	first syllable like 'mat' or like 'mate'?

CHANGE IN SPELLING 6

> English spelling is complex and irregular, and it has only been largely fixed since the eighteenth century. Much of this complexity derives from our custom of spelling words as they were pronounced centuries ago, rather than as they are pronounced now.

The peculiarities of the English spelling system are well known. On the one hand, we have words pronounced identically but spelled differently, such as *flour* and *flower*; on the other hand, we have words spelled identically but pronounced differently, such as *lead* (the metal) and *lead* (the verb). The vowel sound occurring in the word *day* is spelled in an astonishing number of different ways: *day, rain, bass, hate, skein, sleigh, they, gaol, gauge, break, deign, fete, café, ballet, negligee, métier, dahlia, straight, laissez-faire, beaujolais* and *Gaelic*, not to mention the surnames *Hayes, Lehmann, Duquesne* and *Gahagan* – and it's unlikely that this list is exhaustive. On the other hand, the written sequence *-ough* represents a startling variety of sounds in *through, bough, though, bought, cough, rough* and *hiccough*. And there are many words whose spelling may seem downright mysterious, such as *women, debt, one, night, tomb, knife, of, heir, walk, autumn, gnaw, island* and *come*.

What is the reason for our complex and irregular spelling system? Well, there is no single reason: the history of English spelling is a rather complicated affair in which a number of quite distinct developments and influences can be identified. But, as you will already have realized, one of the most important factors has been the operation of language change. In particular, many of our odd-looking spellings are the result of pronunciation change: words like *break, night, one, knife* and *should* have spellings which accurately reflect the way they were pronounced centuries ago. Their pronunciation has changed, but we have never got round to changing their spelling. If we were ever to do this, we might decide to spell these words 'brake', 'nite', 'wun', 'nife' and 'shood'. Indeed, some people have argued for years that just such a modernization of our archaic spelling would be desirable, but so far their arguments have had little effect.

Most people today seem reluctant to consider any modifications in our admittedly perplexing spelling, perhaps because there is now such a vast body of printed works enshrining our conventional spelling and perhaps also because, to anyone who has already made the effort to master the intricacies of the traditional spelling, such 'simplified' spellings as 'nite' and 'shood' look bizarre and illiterate.

Nevertheless, it is perfectly possible for spelling to change, and indeed the spelling of English has changed substantially over the centuries, both in its main lines and in the details of particular words. Sometimes the spelling has changed to represent a genuine change in the pronunciation of a word, as when the Old English spelling *hlæfdige* was eventually changed to *lady* to keep up with the newer pronunciation. In other cases the general spelling conventions of English have been altered, leading to a change of spelling even without any change in pronunciation, as when Old English *cwic* was replaced by *quick*.

As an illustration of the complex history of English spelling, consider the word *shield*. According to the *Oxford English Dictionary*, this word has at various times been spelled *scild, scyld, sceld, seld, sseld, sheld, cheld, scheld, sceild, scheeld, cheeld, schuld, scelde, schild, schilde, schylde, shilde, schelde, sheeld, schield, childe, scheild, scheelde, scheyld, shyld, shulde, shild, shylde, sheelde, shielde, sheild* and *shield*. Only in the late eighteenth century did the last form become fixed as the only possibility; very many other words show a similarly complex history.

EXERCISE

6.0 Below are the Old English spellings of some words whose pronunciation has changed only moderately since the Old English period. How many of them can you recognize? (þ = modern English *th*.)

(a) cwen   (b) heofon
(c) cirice   (d) sceap
(e) niht   (f) geong
(g) tægl   (h) geolu
(i) ofer   (j) dranc
(k) broþor   (l) brycg
(m) sceal   (n) hwæt

Answers

(a) queen   (b) heaven
(c) church   (d) sheep
(e) night   (f) young
(g) tail   (h) yellow

(i) over   (j) drank
(k) brother   (l) bridge
(m) shall   (n) what

These examples illustrate some of the systematic features of Old English spelling which were later replaced by different conventions, such as the use of *cw* for modern *qu*, *c* for both *ch* and *k*, *sc* for *sh*, *g* for *y*, *cg* for *dg* and *hw* for *wh*, as well as the special letters æ (for the vowel of *cat*) and þ (for the sounds now spelled *th*). These and other changes were largely a consequence of the conquest of England by the French-speaking Normans in 1066. For many years after this event, French was used for writing most important documents, and English was comparatively little used for writing. When, after several generations, English came once again to be used as the major written language, scribes felt free to devise such spelling conventions as they saw fit, often under the influence of the spelling conventions of French.

But it was to be many centuries more before a more or less standardized spelling system arose for our language. During the period before the Norman Conquest, the West Saxon dialect used by King Alfred had achieved a prominent position in England, and this West Country variety was increasingly regarded as the standard form to be used in writing English. After the Conquest, however, no single variety of English possessed any particular prestige, and consequently every writer of English was inclined to use his or her own local variety and to spell it in whatever manner he or she liked. As a result, the written form of the language during the Middle Ages was characterized by a degree of variation which would be unthinkable today. Standardization was achieved only very slowly and gradually.

One major factor in the fixing of English spelling was the introduction of printing in the fifteenth century. Faced by a bewildering variety of spellings for a single word, the printers made an effort to reduce the variety by settling on one spelling, or at least on only two or three variants. Unfortunately, perhaps, they often preferred the spellings used in earlier medieval manuscripts, with the result that we have already seen: the spellings of many words were fixed in forms that represented obsolete pronunciations.

A significant but decidedly unhelpful intervention was made in some cases by scholars too eager to identify a connection with Latin. For example, the Old French word *dette* had been borrowed into English in the fourteenth century, and had usually been spelled *dette* or *det* in English. But the French word derives ultimately from Latin *debitum*, and in the sixteenth century learned writers began to favour the novel spelling *debt*, purely in order to show the (very remote) connection with Latin, and this preposterous spelling came to be standardized. Other words whose spellings have been capriciously altered in this way include *doubt* and *receipt*.

By the eighteenth century the standardization of English spelling was well advanced, but still not complete. It was in this century that the great English dictionaries appeared, the most important of which was Dr Samuel Johnson's magisterial work published in 1755. The influence of this dictionary was such that the spellings preferred by Dr Johnson came to be accepted in almost every case as the standard spelling in England. In the United States, however, it was not Johnson's dictionary, but Noah Webster's dictionary of 1828, which largely settled American spelling.

Johnson and Webster did not always make the same choices between competing spellings, and this is the principal reason for the well-known differences between British and American spelling. For example, such words as *theater* and *center* had long been so spelled in England, but in the eighteenth century a fashion arose for using the French spellings *theatre* and *centre*, and it was these novel spellings that were enshrined in Johnson's dictionary and hence in British usage. Webster, in contrast, preferred the traditional spellings, and these have ever since been normal in the United States. Such other British/American differences as *colour/color* and *analyse/analyze* came about in the same way, as differences among competing forms.

SUMMARY

- Modern English spelling is complex and irregular.
- English spelling has been highly variable throughout most of its history; our modern spelling was only more or less fixed in the eighteenth century.
- One important reason for the complexity of our spelling is our frequent practice of spelling words the way they were pronounced centuries ago, without allowing for changes in pronunciation that have occurred.

EXERCISES

6.1 The wide range of spellings used for the vowel sound of *day* was pointed out in the text. How many different spellings can you find for each of the following:

(a) the vowel of *die*;
(b) the vowel of *see*;
(c) the consonant of *key*?

6.2 The letters *u* and *v* were used rather differently in Early Modern English from the way they are used today. Consider the following spellings from the plays of Shakespeare, all written sometime around 1600:

dutie 'duty'
vs 'us'
very 'very'
greeuous 'grievous'

vpon 'upon'
enuy 'envy'
outliue 'outlive'
peruersly 'perversely'
reuennew 'revenue'
thou 'thou'
vp 'up'
villaine 'villain'

What apparently were the rules for using these letters in Shakespeare's day?

6.3 It was stated in the text that one of the main reasons for the complexity of modern English spelling is its conservatism: we often spell words in a way that represents the way they were pronounced centuries ago, and not the way they're pronounced now. But there are other important reasons. Consider the following words, all of which have spellings which are perhaps somewhat unexpected, given their pronunciations:

phoenix, champagne, fete, ski, hymn, machine, chablis, yacht, autumn, Thomas, choir, lasagna, pneumatic, isle, pizza

Why do you suppose we use these odd-looking spellings, instead of more obvious spellings such as 'fenix', 'shampane', 'fate', 'skee', 'him', 'masheen', 'shably', and so on?

6.4 Part of the problem with English spelling is that our alphabet contains only twenty-six letters, whereas the language contains far more than twenty-six distinctive sounds. For this and other reasons, almost every English letter has more than one pronunciation. For example, l is pronounced differently in *life* and *walk*; z is pronounced differently in *zoo* and *pizza*; c is pronounced differently in *call* and *cell*; and so on. See how many different pronunciations you can find for the letters s, u, g and x. Is it possible to find a letter which is pronounced in exactly the same way in every single word in which it occurs?

7 CHANGE IN GRAMMAR

> The grammar of English has changed dramatically in the last thousand years. The most important changes took place centuries ago, but our grammar is continuing to change even today.

In the previous units, we have seen examples of the ways in which language change has resulted in differences of vocabulary and pronunciation among the several varieties of contemporary English. In this unit we shall be looking at the phenomenon of grammatical change.

Differences in grammatical forms between varieties of English are perhaps less conspicuous than differences in vocabulary or pronunciation, but they nevertheless exist. Consider the following two sentences, and decide which seems more natural to you:

(a) My turntable needs the stylus changed.
(b) My turntable needs the stylus changing.

It is likely that you find one of these much more normal than the other. Very roughly, if you live in the southeast of England, in Scotland or in North America, you probably prefer the first form; if you come from the north or the Midlands of England, or from the southwest, you are more likely to prefer the second. (I say 'very roughly', because the distribution of these two forms is rather complex.) Here we have a case in which different regional varieties of English have developed slightly different grammatical forms. Now consider another pair of examples, and decide which you prefer:

(c) The stylus needs changed.
(d) The stylus needs changing.

This time the distribution is different. The (c) form is preferred by most speakers in Scotland and in the western Pennsylvania area of the United States (an area, remember, which was largely settled by people of Scottish origin). All other speakers use the (d) form, and indeed usually find the (c) form startling.

Consider another pair of examples:

(e) She gave it me.
(f) She gave me it.

Which of these is more normal for you? Most speakers in the north of England appear to prefer the (e) form, as do also many southern speakers. Other southerners, and probably most speakers outside England, use only the (f) form. In this case, the historical evidence seems to show rather clearly that the (e) form was once usual for all English speakers; the (f) pattern appears to be an innovation that has appeared in the last two or three centuries.

More surprising examples of grammatical change are not hard to find. The familiar verb *go* formerly had an irregular past-tense form *yede* or *yode*. In about the fifteenth century, however, it acquired a new past-tense form: *went*. Where did this odd-looking form come from? It came from the now rare verb *wend*, which was formerly inflected *wend/went*, just like *send/sent* and *spend/spent*. But the past-tense *went* was detached from *wend* and attached to *go*, which lost its earlier past tense, giving the modern English pattern *go/went*. Meanwhile the verb *wend* has acquired a new past-tense form *wended* (as in *She wended her way home from the party*.)

On the whole, the changes in the grammar of English in the last several centuries have been less than dramatic. At an earlier stage of its history, however, English underwent some changes in its grammar which were decidedly more spectacular and far-reaching. Let us look at some simple examples of Old English.

EXERCISES

7.0 Consider the following sentences of Old English, given here with modern translations (þ = modern English *th*; æ = modern English *a*:)

Se cyning me seah. 'The king saw me.'
Ic seah þone cyning. 'I saw the king.'
Hwæt is þæs cyninges nama? 'What is the king's name?'
Ic hit geaf þæm cyninge. 'I gave it to the king.'
Þa cyningas me sawon. 'The kings saw me.'
Hwæt sind þara cyninga naman? 'What are the kings' names?'
Ic hit geaf þæm cyningum. 'I gave it to the kings.'

In what respects does the grammar of Old English obviously differ from that of Modern English?

Discussion

Most conspicuously, words in Old English changed their form for grammatical purposes far more than occurs in the modern language. So, for example, 'the king' is variously *se cyning* or *þone cyning*, depending on its grammatical role, while 'to the king' is *þæm cyninge* and 'to the kings' is *þæm cyningum*, with the sense of 'to' being expressed by the endings. This kind of grammatical behaviour is found in many other European languages, such as German, Russian and Latin. It was formerly the norm in English, too, but, in the centuries following the Norman Conquest, most of these endings disappeared from the language – and indeed English is today a little unusual among European languages in the small number of grammatical word-endings it uses.

You have probably also noticed that the order of words in Old English is sometimes rather different from the modern order. The placement of pronouns like 'me' and 'it' has particularly changed, and, as the example *She gave it me/She gave me it*, discussed above, shows, some modern varieties have altered the earlier pattern more than others.

It is possible to identify grammatical changes which have been in progress in English for centuries. Let us look at one of these. Consider the following examples:

(a) **Edison invented the electric light.**
(b) **The electric light was invented by Edison.**

Active
Passive

These two constructions are conveniently called the ACTIVE (a) and the PASSIVE (b). From early in the Old English period, the passive construction has existed side by side with the active. For many centuries, however, the passive was limited to occurring in certain very simple types of sentences. In more complex types of sentences, the passive could not be used; this was particularly so with the *-ing* form of the verb. Here are some examples from eighteenth-century English (with modernized spelling, since the spelling is not at issue here):

(c) **I met a dead corpse of the plague, just carrying down a little pair of stairs**

(Samuel Pepys)

(d) **His picture is drawing for me.**

(Samuel Pepys)

(e) **I guessed there was some mischief contriving.**

(Jonathan Swift)

All these were quite normal in the eighteenth century and earlier, but they are very strange now. We would use a passive construction, and say '... just being carried down ...', '... is being drawn ...' and '. . being contrived . . .'. This new kind of passive appeared in the eighteenth century, and at first it was bitterly attacked by linguistic conservatives, who called it 'clumsy', 'illogical', 'confusing' and 'monstrous'. But by the early nineteenth century the new form had established itself even in careful written English, and today hardly anybody would say *My house is painting* or *My car is repairing*; the normal forms are now *My house is being painted* and *My car is being repaired*.

Yet more complex types of sentences have come to permit the passive even more recently. What do you think of the next pair of examples?

(f) They've been painting my house for two weeks now.
(g) My house has been being painted for two weeks now.

The passive illustrated in (g) is newer still; it was hardly used before the twentieth century, and even today many people find sentences like (g) very strange and sometimes even impossible. Perhaps you are one of them.

SUMMARY

- The grammar of English has changed very substantially since the Old English period.
- The most dramatic changes occurred before the end of the Middle Ages, but further changes in grammar are occurring even today.

EXERCISES

7.1 In each of the following pairs of examples, the (a) form is more usual in American English and the (b) form in British English, and the difference is the result of a grammatical innovation on one side of the Atlantic or the other. Can you make a reasonable guess as to where the change has occurred, and why it might have occurred? The first one is done for you.

(1a) I dreamed about you last night.
(1b) I dreamt about you last night.

The form *dreamt* is irregular, and American English has replaced it with the regular form *dreamed*, on the model of regular verbs like *love/loved*.

(2a) I've just gotten my new passport.
(2b) I've just got my new passport.

(3a) She dove into the water.
(3b) She dived into the water.

(4a) We just finished dinner.
(4b) We've just finished dinner.

(5a) You have a cold, don't you?
(5b) You have a cold, haven't you?

(6a) I insisted she take a sweater along.
(6b) I insisted she took a sweater along.

Singular
Plural

7.2 English nouns usually have two different forms called SINGULAR and PLURAL: one *dog* but two *dogs*; one *box* but two *boxes*; and so on. Most nouns behave exactly like *dog* and *box*, but there are a few exceptions: one *foot* but two *feet*; one *child* but two *children*; one *sheep* but two *sheep*. Here are a few English nouns with the plural forms they have had in Old English, Middle English and Modern English; these forms have been considerably simplified to show the general pattern of development. What seems to have been happening to our system for forming plurals?

Singular	Plural: Old English	Middle English	Modern English
book	beek	books	books
child	childer	children	children
cow	ky	kine	cows
egg	eyer	eyren	eggs
eye	eyn	eyen	eyes
fish	fish	fish	fish
foot	feet	feet	feet
hand	handa	handen	hands
man	men	men	men
ox	oxen	oxen	oxen
shoe	shoos	shooen	shoes
word	word	words	words

7.3 Until the middle of the eighteenth century, most speakers of English were happy to speak and write the language just as it came naturally to them. From that time on, however, grammarians began to complain about, and to condemn, particular forms and constructions which they regarded as 'illogical', 'inelegant' or just plain 'wrong', often for no very clear reason beyond their own tastes and prejudices. Here are some examples of the constructions they condemned. All of them were in fact perfectly normal in English before the grammarians set to work. How do you find these examples now?

(a) I will be there at eight o'clock.
(b) The one you want is me.
(c) I don't have no money.
(d) That's the man I was talking to.
(e) I need to really make an effort.
(f) Who did you see?

7.4 The English of Shakespeare's plays includes a number of grammatical forms and constructions which are no longer normal in standard English. Here are some quotations from Shakespeare; how would you render them in modern English? (Shakespeare's spelling, which is not at issue here, has been silently modernized.)

(a) What says he of our marriage?
(b) Where is thy husband now? Where be thy brothers?
(c) 'Tis known to you he is mine enemy ...
    And no great friend, I fear me, to the King.
(d) The common executioner ...
    Falls not the axe upon the humbled neck.
(e) His lordship is walked forth into the orchard.
(f) The clock struck nine, when I did send the nurse.
(g) I care not.
(h) Sometimes she driveth over a soldier's neck, and then
    dreams he of cutting foreign throats.

CHANGE IN MEANING 8

> Like other aspects of language, the meanings of words can change over time. Two common types of change are broadening and narrowing of meaning, but many other types can occur.

On a Sunday in 1948, the Princess Elizabeth (now Queen Elizabeth II) gave birth to a son, Charles, the future Prince of Wales. One member of the House of Lords chose to celebrate the occasion by quoting a nineteenth-century nursery rhyme:

The child that is born on the Sabbath day
Is fair and wise, and good and gay.

It is most unlikely that any future royal births will be commemorated in quite this way: even the most barnacle-encrusted peer would probably now be reluctant to describe the heir to the throne as 'gay'.

In 1948, the word 'gay' had, in everyday usage, only its traditional meaning of 'cheerful', 'lively'. But in the 1950s this word began to be used as a synonym for *homosexual*, and that is now its most usual sense: if someone tells you *John is gay*, you will probably understand 'John is homosexual', not 'John is cheerful'. Since 1948, the word *gay* has changed its meaning rather radically.

Like pronunciation, like grammar, like spelling, like vocabulary, like every aspect of language, the meanings of words can and do change with time. We have already seen a few other examples of this in English: recall that in **Unit 2** we met Chaucer using the word *villainy* in its earlier sense of 'lack of good breeding'; today, this word means 'evil-doing'.

In fact, all of the words *villain*, *churl* and *boor* once meant nothing more than 'farm worker'. Today all three are insults, a development perhaps reflecting the city slicker's habitual contempt for his or her unsophisticated rural cousins. The word *peasant* is now going the same way: though we can still speak of third-world farmers as 'peasants' without intending any slight, we can equally say *You peasant!*, meaning 'You uncultured lout!'

Needless to say, English words have been changing their meanings throughout the history of the language. Some of the changes which have occurred are easy to understand, while others are quite surprising. Here are a few examples: *girl* formerly meant 'young person (of either sex)'; *meat* formerly meant 'food (of any kind)'; *dog* was formerly the name of a particular breed of dog. Both *knave* and *knight* once meant 'boy' or 'servant', but their meanings have not only changed, but changed in opposite directions. More surprising are the cases of *jaw*, which formerly meant 'cheek', and *cheek*, which formerly meant 'jaw'! (And it is thought that the word *chin* probably once meant 'cheek' as well.)

Specialization
Generalization

The examples of *girl* and *meat* illustrate what linguists call SPECIALIZATION: the meaning of a word becomes less general than formerly. The opposite development, GENERALIZATION, is illustrated by *dog*. Both of these appear to be particularly common types of change in meaning.

In Spanish, the word *caballo* means 'horse', and *caballero*, which is derived from it, apparently means 'horseman'. However, when you visit Spain, you will see public toilets marked *Caballeros*, but you are hardly likely to observe any horsemen attempting to ride into them, or even up to them. *Caballero* did indeed mean 'horseman' once, but, since only people of an elevated social class could afford to ride horses, the word came to mean 'man of quality', 'gentleman' (in the older sense of this English word); today *caballero* is simply a polite word for 'man', just like English 'gentleman', which has similarly enlarged its meaning.

Euphemism

One of the most fertile sources of new meanings is the creation of EUPHEMISMS – polite but roundabout expressions for things which are considered too nasty to talk about directly. When indoor plumbing began to be installed in houses in the eighteenth century, the new little room installed for private purposes was at first called a *water closet*, soon abbreviated to *WC*. Eventually this term came to be regarded as intolerably blunt, and it was variously replaced by *toilet* (which had previously meant simply 'dressing table') or *lavatory* (a Latin word meaning 'place for washing'). Today these words in turn are regarded as unbearably crude by many people, and yet further euphemisms have been pressed into service: the usual American word is now *bathroom* (the toilet and the bath are usually in the same room in an American house), and an American child who says *I gotta go to the bathroom* is definitely not looking for a bath.

Sex is another area in which euphemisms flourish. In the nineteenth century, the novelist Jane Austen could write of the very genteel Miss Anne Elliott and her haughty neighbour Captain Wentworth that 'they had no intercourse but what the commonest civility required'. The author would have been dumbfounded by the effect of this sentence on a modern reader: in her time, of course, the word *intercourse* meant nothing more than 'dealings between people'. In the twentieth century, however, the phrase *sexual intercourse* was created as a very delicate way of talking about copulation; this has now been shortened to *intercourse*, and this sexual sense is now so prevalent that we find it impossible to use the word in any other sense at all.

EXERCISE

8.0 How many euphemisms can you find for each of the following words and phrases?

- (a) to die
- (b) to urinate
- (c) to be a sexual partner of
- (d) to kill

Here are a few of the many euphemisms which are or have been used; doubtless you have thought of others.

Discussion

- (a) to die: to pass away, to go west, to kick the bucket, to be no longer with us, to expire, to buy the farm, to buy it, to slip away, to give up the ghost;
- (b) to urinate: to pass water, to relieve oneself, to have a wee, to do number one, to water the daisies, to powder one's nose, to see a man about a dog;
- (c) to be a sexual partner of: to sleep with, to be seeing, to be going out with, to be a close friend of, to be on intimate terms with;
- (d) to kill: to liquidate, to terminate (with extreme prejudice), to remove, to eliminate, to dispose of, to rub out, to hit.

SUMMARY

- Like all other aspects of language, the meanings of words can change over time.
- Two particular common types of meaning change are specialization (limitation of meaning) and generalization (broadening of meaning).
- Another frequent type of meaning change results from the seemingly constant need to provide new euphemisms in place of words regarded as unpleasantly blunt.

EXERCISES

8.1 Each of the following sentences should seem normal enough. However, in each case, the modern meaning of the word in italics is quite different from its earlier meaning, and the sentence would be quite impossible if the word had retained its original meaning. Try to guess the earlier meaning of the word from the context, and check your guess in a good dictionary which provides earlier meanings or in the appendix to this book.

44 CHANGE IN MEANING

(a) No animals are allowed in the *cockpit*.
(b) Miss Marple's knitting wool cannot be a *clue*.
(c) The *candidate* turned up in a dark blue suit.
(d) She is small and slim, but she has a great deal of *poise*.
(e) We *arrived* at a dusty village in the middle of the desert.
(f) Wrapping her cloak tightly about her, she *escaped* from her escort.
(g) Japanese *manufacturers* make heavy use of automated factories.
(h) The ship's passengers were *quarantined* for two weeks.
(i) John is a *mediocre* mountain-climber, but he always makes it to the top.
(j) After the break-in, our vegetarian shop was a *shambles*.
(k) She's painted a lovely blue-and-yellow *miniature*.
(l) A *dishevelled* old man, bald and toothless, huddled in a doorway.

8.2 In some cases, the change in meaning of a word can only be understood in terms of associated cultural changes or particular historical events. Here are a few examples of such words. Consulting a good dictionary or the appendix to this book where necessary, try to explain the changes in the meanings of these words.

(a) The word *car* derives from Latin **carra* 'two-wheeled cart'.
(b) The words *electron*, *electronics* and *electricity* all derive from Greek *elektron* 'amber' (petrified tree resin).
(c) The word *book* is derived from the name of the *beech* tree.
(d) The word *chapel* is derived from Latin *cappella* 'cloak'.
(e) The word *money* derives from Latin *moneta* 'one who admonishes'.
(f) The word *sinister* derives from Latin *sinister* 'on the left-hand side'.
(g) The names of *September* and *October*, the ninth and tenth months of the year, are derived from Latin *septem* 'seven' and *octo* 'eight'.
(h) The word *charm* derives from Latin *carmen* 'song'.

Metaphor

8.3 Very often a phrase or expression with a highly specific meaning comes to be used as a METAPHOR and hence to be used in a much wider sense. Here are a few examples, all of nautical origin. Consulting a good dictionary or the appendix to this book where necessary, explain the shift in meaning.

(a) There'll be the devil to pay.
(b) He nailed his colours to the mast.
(c) We're in the doldrums.
(d) I didn't like the cut of his jib.
(e) The opportunity has gone by the board.

(f) We gave him a wide berth.
(g) She took the wind out of his sails.

8.4 On the left is a list of words which have undergone substantial changes of meaning during the last few centuries; on the right is a list of their former meanings in a different order. Can you match each word with its former meaning?

(a) *sack*   (1) 'understanding'
(b) *prove*   (2) 'monk's costume'
(c) *skill*   (3) 'foolish'
(d) *disease*   (4) 'unrelated'
(e) *frock*   (5) 'feather'
(f) *wade*   (6) 'test'
(g) *thing*   (7) 'strong wine'
(h) *silly*   (8) 'time'
(i) *reek*   (9) 'discomfort'
(j) *impertinent* (10) 'prayer'
(k) *fee*   (11) 'livestock'
(l) *boon*   (12) 'legal matter'
(m) *pen*   (13) 'smoke'
(n) *tide*   (14) 'go'
(o) *fond*   (15) 'helpless'

9 THE ORIGIN OF DIALECTS

> The combination of language change and geographical separation inevitably results in the rise of regional dialects; if no unifying force intervenes, dialects may diverge from one another without limit.

The ancestral form of English was brought to Britain from the fifth century onwards, by peoples migrating from the northwest of the continent of Europe, from areas that are now part of the Netherlands, Germany and Denmark. These peoples were variously known as Angles, Saxons, Jutes and Frisians. They spoke closely related dialects of a language which seems to have had no generally accepted name at the time; after their settlement in Britain, the name of one of these peoples eventually came to be applied to the language spoken by all of them: Anglish, or English.

For the first several centuries of the English settlement of Britain, we have no significant written records of the language. By the early eighth century, however, English was beginning to be written in a form of the Roman alphabet; by the ninth and tenth centuries, writing in English was voluminous, and very many English texts from this period have survived down to the present day.

One of the most striking features of these texts is the significant differences in the way English was written in different parts of the country. These differences largely reflect differences in the way the language was spoken. That is, in the space of three or four centuries, significant dialect differences had arisen in English. This is hardly surprising. In an age when travel was mostly on foot, or occasionally on horseback, and no message could be sent faster than a human being could carry it, communication between widely separated areas was slow and infrequent. As a result, linguistic changes appearing in one part of the country could spread only very slowly, and three or four centuries was ample time for the accumulated weight of such changes to bring about substantial regional differences in English. (For comparison, American English has had scarcely three centuries to diverge from British English, and Australian English rather less than two centuries.)

Scholars recognize four main groups of dialects of Old English: Northumbrian (spoken in northern England and southern Scotland), Mercian (in the Midlands), West Saxon (in the southwest) and Kentish (in the southeast). Superimposed on these four main groupings, moreover, were innumerable local differences. For illustration, here is an extract from a famous Old English poem, the celebrated *Hymn* of the poet Caedmon, in two dialects. The first version is Northumbrian, the second West Saxon (þ = modern English *th*; æ = modern English *a*):

(1) Nu scylan hergan hefænrices uard
 metudæs mæcti end his modgidanc
 uerc uuldorfadur sue he uundra gihuæs
 eci dryctin or astelidæ.
(2) Nu sculon herigean heofonrices weard
 meotodes meahte & his modgeþanc
 weorc wuldorfæder swa he wundra gehwæs
 ece drihten or onstealde.

To some extent, the apparent differences in the two versions merely reflect different local spelling conventions, but mostly they represent genuine differences in the way English was spoken.

English has now been spoken in Britain for well over a thousand years, and the same slow but steady processes of language change have continued to operate throughout this period. Throughout the Middle Ages, regional differences continued to develop, and by the fifteenth century, it is clear, English speakers from different parts of the country often had great difficulty in understanding one another.

EXERCISE

9.0 If nothing had happened to transform this situation, what would have been the likely result of this steady divergence among regional varieties of English? In fact, what did happen to produce a very different result?

Discussion

If nothing had intervened, it is quite possible that English, both in Britain and elsewhere, might have broken up into several mutually incomprehensible languages. (In fact, some scholars seriously maintain even today that the English of Scotland, and perhaps also the English of the United States, should be regarded as different languages from the English of England – a position which seems unnecessarily extreme.)

But several factors intervened. First, there were political factors. Moves toward the political unification of Britain, and the increasing prestige of the capital city, London, and of the universities in Oxford and Cambridge, meant that the kind of English spoken in this part of the country was also increasingly seen as prestigious. Consequently, speakers from other parts of the country were often eager to use this variety of English, particularly for writing, or at least to adjust their speech towards what gradually came to be seen as a national standard.

More recently, the historic trend towards regional fragmentation has been overtaken by spectacular developments in transport and communication. Thanks to the introduction of trains, cars, planes, films, radio, television and recordings, speakers of English now have constant and rapid access to the English spoken, not just elsewhere in Britain, but anywhere else in the world. Today, if a new word becomes fashionable in California, English speakers in Wigan, Ipswich and Sydney are likely to hear about it in a matter of weeks. This is a far cry from the days when an English speaker only rarely encountered the English spoken fifty miles away.

After many centuries of slow divergence among regional varieties of English, the tendency is now largely the other way: towards a levelling of English everywhere, and a reduction in regional diversity. But this process is far from complete, and there is little reason to suppose that regional differences will ever disappear completely. Major regional differences are still with us, and speakers from, say, Glasgow, Newcastle, Liverpool and Southampton can sometimes find it exasperatingly difficult to carry on a conversation.

SUMMARY

- English has been characterized by dialect differences from its earliest days.
- Dialect differences are the inevitable result of language change combined with geographical separation.
- The natural tendency of dialects to grow further apart can be resisted by such factors as political unity and efficient communication.
- In the absence of such resisting factors, dialects may diverge with time into completely different languages.

EXERCISES

9.1 Literary writers have often attempted to represent particular regional dialects in their novels and poems. Here are a few examples. Can you identify the dialect which the author is trying to portray in each case?

(a) Lock, lock! How skittish we be now! Yow weren't zo skittish wey Kester Hosegood up to Daraty Vuzz's upzetting – no, no, yow weren't zo skittish then, ner zo squemesh nether, HE murt muly and soully tell ha wos weary.

(b) Meä an' thy sister was married, when wer it? back-end o' June,
Ten years sin', and wa 'greed as well as a fiddle i' tune:
I could fettle and clump owd booöts and shoes wi' the best on 'em all,
As fer as fro' Thursby thurn hup to Harmsby and Hutterby Hall.

(c) 'Appen yer'd better 'ave this key, an' Ah mun fend for t'bods some other road . . . I mean as 'appen Ah can find anuther pleece as'll du for rearin' th' pheasants. If yer want to be 'ere, you'll no want me messin' abaht a' th' time.

(d) But to our tale, Ae market night,
Tam had got planted unco right,
Feast by an ingle, bleezing finely,
Wi' reaming swats, that drank divinely.

9.2 Like Britain, the United States exhibits some notable regional dialects. It is not difficult to distinguish the speech of, say, New England, New York City, West Virginia and Mississippi. However, the regional differences in the United States are much less marked than those in Britain, and moreover they are almost entirely confined to the eastern and southeastern parts of the country. Dialect differences in most of the rest of the country are so slight that even Americans are scarcely aware of them. Why should this be so?

9.3 Major cities often develop fairly distinctive speech varieties of their own: think of Newcastle or Birmingham. But, if you travel away from Newcastle or Birmingham, you will find that speech patterns change only rather gradually as you move into the surrounding territory. Noticeably different are the cases of Liverpool and New York: each of these cities has a famously distinctive local speech variety of its own, and, if you travel away from either of them, you will find a comparatively abrupt change from the distinct urban variety to something obviously different. What is special about Liverpool and New York that they should have such distinctive and localized speech?

9.4 The ancestral form of English was brought to Britain from the Continent by the Angles, Saxons, Jutes and Frisians. But, of course, not all of the speakers of ancestral English emigrated to Britain: many remained on the Continent. What happened to their 'English'?

RELATEDNESS BETWEEN LANGUAGES 10

> Given sufficient time, the ordinary processes of language can split a single language not merely into dialects but into distinct languages. Languages which share a common origin of this kind are said to be genetically related. English is genetically related to a group of languages collectively known as the Germanic languages.

In the last unit we stressed the point that, with the passage of time, a single more-or-less homogeneous language tends to split into different regional varieties. Given sufficient time, these DIALECTS (regional varieties) can diverge so much that they eventually become mutually incomprehensible and must at some point be regarded as different LANGUAGES. This has never quite happened to English: political and other forces have been sufficient to resist the fragmentation into different languages which might otherwise have occurred.

Dialect

Language

But recall that there were a number of speakers of ancestral English who never crossed the North Sea to Britain. They remained on the Continent, and their speech was never subjected to the influences which determined the course followed by English in Britain. As centuries of language change accumulated, with different changes occurring on both sides of the North Sea, the language of the English and the language of their kinsmen in Europe continued to diverge. Moreover, as a result of political and other developments in Europe, the ancestral English spoken there split up even more dramatically than was the case in England. Today, the people of the eastern coast of the North Sea speak several quite different languages: Dutch, Frisian, German and Danish. Fifteen hundred years ago, all these peoples spoke the same language as their kinsmen who were beginning to settle in England; today an English speaker can no more understand Dutch or Danish than he or she can understand Polish or

Rumanian. This is a powerful demonstration of the effect of language change combined with geographical separation.

Now notice something interesting. Around 1,500 years ago, the various peoples around the North Sea coast were all speaking closely related dialects of a single language. If this language had a name, it has not survived; modern scholars, for convenience, call it 'Ingvaeonic'. Now Ingvaeonic was a single language, but, with the passage of time, it has split up into several distinct languages, including English, Dutch and Frisian (Frisian is a language spoken on several islands off the coast of the Netherlands, Germany and Denmark). That is, these quite distinct modern languages all started off as nothing more than dialects of a single language. Such splitting of a single language into several different languages is the inevitable result of language change combined with geographical separation, whenever there are insufficient unifying forces to resist this tendency to split.

Genetic relations

English, Frisian and Dutch are therefore said to be GENETICALLY RELATED – that is, they all descend from a common ancestor. One of the most striking successes of modern linguistics is the demonstration that many languages are genetically related in just such a way. In fact,

Family

English, Frisian and Dutch are just three of a much larger FAMILY of languages all of which are descended from a group of closely related dialects spoken in northern Europe around 2,500 years or so ago. Others include Icelandic, Norwegian, Danish, Swedish, Faroese (in the Faroe Islands), German, Yiddish, Afrikaans (in South Africa) and Gothic (an extinct language formerly spoken by many of the barbarian peoples who invaded the Roman Empire). All of these

Germanic

related languages are called the GERMANIC languages, since the peoples who spoke their ancestral forms were collectively known to the Romans as *Germani*. Let us briefly illustrate the genetic relationship among these languages.

EXERCISE

10.0 Consider the following words from English and German. In each case the words have related, though not always identical, meanings. What do you observe, and how can your observations be explained? (German *z* is pronounced like English *ts*.)

English	German	English	German
tongue	Zunge	town	Zaun
tide	Zeit	tile	Ziegel
tin	Zinn	tear	Zähre
token	Zeichen	toll	Zoll
timber	Zimmer	to	zu
twenty	zwanzig	tug	Zug
ten	zehn	tinder	Zünder
tell	zählen	tap	Zapfen
twig	Zweig		

The words are often very similar in form, but this is not the most interesting point. More important is the following: whenever an English word begins with *t*, the corresponding German word, with a high degree of consistency, begins with *z* (that is, with *ts*). This kind of pattern is called a SYSTEMATIC CORRESPONDENCE, and there is only one way of explaining its presence. At some time in the past, English and German must have been no more than dialects of a single language, and all these words were present in that ancestral language and happened to begin with the same sound. That sound, whatever it was, has become a *t* in English but a *z* in German, very regularly. At least one of these two languages, therefore, must have undergone a significant change in pronunciation since the time when the two dialects split. (In fact, linguists are sure that these words all began with a *t* in the ancestral language, and that the pronunciation of this sound has therefore changed in German but not in English.)

Discussion

Systematic correspondence

Note carefully that it is the *pattern* which is important here, and not just the obvious similarities. Similarities between languages can have many explanations, including chance coincidence, but systematic correspondences can only result from a genetic relationship.

In fact, the historical connections between English and German can be easily demonstrated in a variety of ways. Consider, for example, the behaviour of verbs in the two languages:

English	**German**
laugh–laughed	lachen–lachte
hate–hated	hassen–haste
love–loved	lieben–liebte
think–thought	denken–dachte
bring–brought	bringen–brachte
sing–sang–sung	singen–sang–gesungen
give–gave–given	geben–gab–gegeben
fall–fell–fallen	fallen–fiel–gefallen

Both the regular and the irregular patterns of English are matched faithfully in German, something which can only be explained if both languages inherited these patterns from their common ancestor. The other Germanic languages show similar patterns, reflecting their descent from the same ancestor.

And what can we say about this ancestral language? Well, the term 'Ingvaeonic' applies only to the closely related dialects spoken around the North Sea. Other, somewhat less closely related, dialects were already being spoken by the fifth century to the north and east of the Ingvaeonic group. Linguistic scholars trace all of these dialects back to a single ancestral language which they call PROTO-GERMANIC (the name means the 'first' or 'earliest' Germanic language). Who spoke Proto-Germanic, and where and when? This is not so easy to answer, since the speakers of Proto-Germanic had not acquired

Proto-Germanic

writing, and so they left no written texts for us to study. But the consensus at present is that Proto-Germanic was probably spoken in southern Scandinavia in about the middle of the first millennium BC. Its speakers, of whom we know little, soon began to spread out from this homeland. By the fifth century AD, speakers of the gradually diverging Germanic dialects had spread over a large area of Europe, ranging from Norway in the north to southern Russia in the east to Italy and Spain in the south, and of course some of them were beginning to move into Britain. In most of eastern and southern Europe, the Germanic languages did not survive, but in central and northern Europe, including Britain, Germanic languages are still spoken today.

By the tenth century or so, many of these Germanic languages were being written down, and enough texts have survived that we know a good deal about the nature of the languages at this time. It is clear that the various dialects had already diverged considerably into what we can reasonably regard as separate languages, though the differences among them were not as great as they are now, a thousand years later. As an example, here are the first three lines of the Lord's Prayer in five Germanic languages, all five versions dating from around the tenth century. Old Saxon was spoken in northwestern Germany and Holland, Old High German in southern Germany, Old Icelandic in Iceland, and Gothic in eastern Europe. (The symbol *uu* represents *w* (of course!), while *þ* represents *th*.)

> *Old English:* Fæder ure þu þe eart in heofuna, si þin nama gehalgod. Tobecume þin rice. Geweorþe þin willa on eorþan swa swa on heofunum.
> *Old Saxon:* Fader usa, thu bist an them himila rikea. Geuuihid si thin namo. Cuma thin riki. Uuertha thin uuilleo, so sama an ertho, so an them himilo rikea.
> *Old High German:* Fater unser, thu in himilon bist, geuuihit si namo thin. Quaeme richi thin. Uuerdhe uuilleo thin, sama so in himile endi in erdu.
> *Old Icelandic:* Faþer várr sa þú ert i hifne, helgesk nafn þitt. Til kome þitt rike. Verþe þinn vile, suá a iorþ sem a hifne.
> *Gothic:* Atta unsar þu in himinamn weihnai namo þein. Qimai þiudinassus þeins. Waírþai wilja þeins, swe in himina jah ana aírþai.
> *Early Modern English:* Our father, who art in heaven, hallowed be thy name. Thy kingdom come. Thy will be done, on earth as in heaven.

Even from these brief examples, it can be seen that Gothic, linguistically as well as geographically, is the most remote from Old English. But all are very similar, though the similarity is slightly disguised by the use of different spelling conventions. All but Gothic have something like *fader* for 'father'; all have something like *thu* and *thin* ('thou' and 'thine') for 'you' and 'your'; all but Gothic have something like *rike* for 'kingdom'; all have something like *(ge)werthe* for 'be done'; and so on.

We have now briefly traced the history of English back to an unidentified, illiterate people inhabiting Scandinavia some 2,500 years ago. Over centuries, these people slowly spread out over much of Europe, taking their Germanic language with them. As they spread, the remorseless processes of language change brought about ever greater differences among the Germanic dialects, until, by the tenth century or so, we are forced to regard the various Germanic peoples as speaking distinct languages. During the last ten centuries the differences among the Germanic languages have continued to grow, so that today an English speaker finds German or Swedish perhaps no easier to learn than a non-Germanic language like Spanish or Greek.

SUMMARY

- The ordinary processes of language change can, with time, split a single language into a number of quite distinct languages.
- Languages which are derived from a common ancestor in this way are said to be *genetically related*.
- English, German, Swedish and many other European languages are genetically related, since all are descended from a common ancestor called 'Proto-Germanic'.

EXERCISES

10.1 Here are the numerals from one to ten, plus 100, in English and German:

English	German
one	eins
two	zwei
three	drei
four	vier
five	fünf
six	sechs
seven	sieben
eight	acht
nine	neun
ten	zehn
hundred	hundert

And here are the same numerals in a few other European languages, ancient and modern. Can you tell which of these languages are Germanic from the numerals alone? (Be careful! Some of the non-Germanic languages look suspiciously similar to the Germanic ones, for a reason to be explained in the next unit.) Special symbols: ç and č = English *ch*; ş and š = English *sh*; þ = modern English *th*.

A	B	C	D
en	uno	bir	un
to	due	iki	dau
tre	tre	üç	tri
fire	quattro	dört	pedwar
fem	cinque	beş	pump
seks	sei	altï	chwech
syv	sette	yedi	saith
otte	otto	sekiz	wyth
ni	nove	dokuz	naw
ti	dieci	on	deg
honderd	cento	yüz	cant

E	F	G	H
bat	een	an	edin
bi	twee	twegen	dva
hiru	drie	þry	tri
lau	vier	feower	četiri
bost	vijf	fif	pet
sei	zes	syx	šest
zazpi	zeven	seofon	sedem
zortzi	acht	eahta	osem
bederatzi	negen	nigon	devet
hamar	tien	tyn	deset
ehun	honderd	hundteontig	sto

10.2 In the text I pointed out the systematic correspondence between English *t* and German *z* at the beginning of a word. Here are some more related English and German words (again, the meanings are similar but not necessarily identical). See if you can find some further systematic correspondences, not necessarily at the beginnings of words.

English	German	English	German
apple	Apfel	go	geh(en)
bear	Bär	good	gut
bed	Bett	great	gross
better	besser	green	grün
bid	biet(en)	new	neu
by	bei	nine	neun
day	Tag	pan	Pfanne
door	Tür	penny	Pfennig
dream	Traum	plum	Pflaume
drive	treib(en)	thick	dick
drop	Tropfe	thin	dünn
finger	Finger	think	denk(en)
fire	Feuer	through	durch
foot	Fuss	thumb	Daumen
for	für	water	Wasser
give	geb(en)	white	weiss

Here are some examples. Whenever an English word contains a *t* in the middle or at the end, the corresponding German word has ss in the same position: *better/besser*; *foot/Fuss*; etc. And whenever an English word has an *n* in any position, the corresponding German word also has an *n* there (or occasionally *nn*): *new/neu*; *thin/dünn*; etc.

10.3 Here are some forms of the verb 'to help' in modern Dutch, modern German, Old English and modern English. What do these forms suggest about the earlier Germanic languages and about the history of English? (Old English þ and ð represent modern *th*.)

Dutch	ik help	wij helpen
	jij helpt	jullie helpen
	hij helpt	zij helpen
German	ich helfe	wir helfen
	du hilfst	ihr helft
	er hilft	sie helfen
Old English	ic helpe	we helpað
	þu hilpst	ge helpað
	he hilpð	hi helpað
Modern English	I help	we help
	you help	you help
	he helps	they help

10.4 (for discussion) English is in many ways the odd one out among the modern Germanic languages. As the last exercise suggests, it has arguably undergone more dramatic changes in grammar than its relatives, and there is no doubt at all that it has experienced vastly greater changes in its vocabulary than any other Germanic language. Can you think of any reason why English should have changed more rapidly than its relatives?

11 MORE REMOTE RELATIONS

> The Germanic family of languages to which English belongs is itself only one branch of a much larger family called the Indo-European family. All the languages in this family are descended from a single remote ancestor called Proto-Indo-European, spoken perhaps 6,000 years ago in eastern Europe.

In the last unit we saw that English belongs to the Germanic family of languages. That is, English started off as no more than one of several dialects of the (unrecorded) language we call Proto-Germanic; over time, these dialects diverged into a number of distinct languages, including English, Dutch, German, Danish and many others.

However, this is not the whole story. When you were doing the exercise with the numerals in the last unit, you probably noticed that some other European languages, although not Germanic, nevertheless exhibited some interesting similarities to the Germanic languages. There is a good reason for this. To see what it is, let us begin by considering some data from just two languages, English and Spanish (Spanish is definitely not a Germanic language).

EXERCISE

11.0 Here are some English and Spanish words of very similar meanings. What do you observe when you examine them? What conclusions can you draw, if any?

English	Spanish	English	Spanish
fish	pez	six	seis
for	por	seven	siete
father	padre	sun	sol
foot	pie	sweet	suave
first	primero	-self	se

English	Spanish	English	Spanish
night	noche	heart	corazón
new	nuevo	head	cabeza
nine	nueve	hair	cabello
nose	nariz	hundred	ciento
no	no	horn	cuerno

What you see looks like a set of systematic correspondences of the type discussed in the last unit for the Germanic languages. It appears that English *f-* corresponds to Spanish *p-*, English *s-* to Spanish *s-*, English *n-* to Spanish *n-*, and English *h-* to Spanish *c-*. With such a small set of data, we could, of course, be seeing nothing more than a few chance coincidences. But exhaustive investigation by scholars has demonstrated beyond all dispute that these are not coincidences. Spanish and English are genetically related. But Spanish is not a Germanic language, and the historical connection between English and Spanish is far more remote than that between, say, English and German, or English and Swedish. Nevertheless, it is clear that the ancestors of English and Spanish, long, long ago, were merely dialects of a single language.

Discussion

Before we pursue further the connection between English and Spanish, let us first note that Spanish has much closer relatives than English. The French words for 'fish', 'for', 'father', 'foot' and 'first', for example, are *poisson, pour, père, pied* and *premier*, respectively, while those for 'night', 'new', 'nine', 'nose' and 'no' are *nuit, neuf, neuf, nez* and *non* – far closer to the Spanish forms than to the English. While English, Swedish, German, and so on belong to the Germanic family of languages, Spanish and French, together with a number of other languages, belong to another group, called the Romance languages. Some of the more important Romance languages are Spanish, Catalan and Galician (all spoken in Spain), Portuguese (in Portugal), French and Occitan (in France), Romansh (in part of Switzerland), Italian, Sardinian and Friulian (in Italy) and Rumanian (in Rumania).

All of these Romance languages are related in just the same way as the Germanic languages: they started off around 1,500 or so years ago as no more than the regional dialects of a single ancestral language. Just as the unrecorded ancestor of the Germanic languages is called 'Proto-Germanic', we can refer to the ancestor of the Romance languages as 'Proto-Romance'. But there is one important difference: while Proto-Germanic was never written down, the speakers of Proto-Romance knew how to write, and they have left us large numbers of texts written in their language. That language is the one we more usually call Latin. In other words, Spanish, French, Italian and the rest are all nothing more than the modern regional dialects of Latin.

But what about the English–Spanish connection claimed above? Well, you can probably guess how it arises. English started off as a dialect of Proto-Germanic; Spanish started off as a dialect of Latin. But Proto-Germanic and Latin themselves started out, very much earlier, as dialects of an even earlier language. Moreover, Proto-Germanic and Latin do not by any means represent the only branches of this very early language. Almost all the modern languages of Europe, and also many of the languages of Asia, can trace their origin back to this same ancestral language. This includes the Celtic languages like Irish and Welsh, the Slavic languages like Russian, Polish and Serbo-Croatian, the Iranian languages like Persian and Kurdish, and the north Indian languages like Hindi, Gujerati and Urdu, as well as a number of others: Albanian, Lithuanian, Greek and Armenian, to name just a few.

All these languages and many others represent the modern developments of what was aeons ago a single language. With the passage of time, the remorseless processes of linguistic change caused this language to split up into a number of dialects, which themselves then split into dialects, and so on. Today it is scarcely possible to recognize that English, Greek, Russian and Hindi were once merely dialects of a single language, on a par with the various dialects of English spoken at present, so great has been the accumulation of changes. But nearly two centuries of scholarly investigation has proved beyond any possible doubt that this is so.

Indo-European
Proto-Indo-European (PIE)

Since this great group of languages extends from India to western Europe, we call it the INDO-EUROPEAN family. And the remote ancestor of the Indo-European languages is, of course, called PROTO-INDO-EUROPEAN, or PIE for short.

Who spoke PIE, and where and when? Naturally, these questions have long excited the curiosity of scholars. Linguists are satisfied that PIE must have been spoken between 5,000 and 6,000 years ago, to allow sufficient time for the development of the huge range of modern languages. But the who and the where are far more difficult questions, since the speakers of PIE did not have writing. At present, we simply don't know who spoke PIE or where, but there are several plausible hypotheses. The most popular view is that PIE was spoken in southern Russia, possibly by a people whose remains have been found

Kurgan

by archaeologists and who are called the KURGAN culture. Another view, less widely accepted, is that PIE was spoken in what is now Turkey. There are still other proposals, and we may never know for certain. But what is not in doubt is that PIE was once spoken somewhere, by somebody, and that hundreds of the ancient and modern languages of Europe and Asia have developed from it by the same slow processes of linguistic change that we have been considering in this book.

Of course, not all languages are Indo-European – far from it. Linguists have succeeded in identifying many other important language families comparable to Indo-European, in that all the languages in each one are descended from a single common ancestor. Among these are Sino-Tibetan (including Chinese, Tibetan and Burmese, among many others), Uralic (Finnish, Estonian, Lappish, Hungarian and many Siberian languages), Afro-Asiatic (Arabic, Hebrew, Ancient Egyptian, the Hausa language of Nigeria, and very many others), Ge-Pano-Carib (many languages of South America and the Caribbean), Niger-Congo (the vast majority of sub-Saharan African languages), Australian (virtually all of the aboriginal languages of Australia), Austronesian (most of the languages of Madagascar, Indonesia, Taiwan, the Philippines and the Pacific), and Algonkian (many languages of North America) – to name just a few of the larger families.

SUMMARY

- English is genetically related to a vast number of other languages besides the Germanic ones, though not so closely.
- The family to which English belongs is called the Indo-European family, and all the Indo-European languages are descended from a single remote ancestor called Proto-Indo-European (PIE).
- PIE was never written down, and we can do little more than make educated guesses about who spoke it, and where, and when.
- Indo-European is just one of a large number of language families, though it happens today to be the biggest one.

EXERCISES

11.1 Look again at the numerals in A–H of **Exercise 10.1** in the last unit. Which of the eight languages exemplified there do not appear to be Indo-European?

11.2 We have seen that, with time, a language tends to break up into distinct regional varieties; these varieties slowly become more and more different from one another, until eventually we have to regard them as separate languages. But when is this point reached?

Below are two proverbs rendered into the local speech varieties of eight places between Paris and Madrid; the first means 'The daughter of the cat catches mice', and the second 'As the goat, so the kid' (i.e., 'Like father, like son'). Which of these eight varieties appear to be genetically related? Which are most closely related? Is it possible to decide how many distinct languages are represented?

    A. 1. Fille de chat prend les souris.
       2. Filha de ca pren li gàri.
       3. Filla de gat agafa ratolins.
       4. Hilhe de gat que gahe sourits.
       5. Hilho de gat que gaho es souris.

6. Filla de gato pilla ratòns.
7. Hija de gato coge ratones.
8. Gatu umeak saguak hartzen.

B. 1. Comme est la chèvre, ainsi vient le chevreau.
2. Coum' es la cabra, ansin vèn lou cabrit.
3. Tal com és la cabra, aixì és el cabrit.
4. Tàu coum' èy la crabe, que bat lou crabòt.
5. Coum' éy era crapo, atàu que bat ec crabòt.
6. Como yé la craba, asi será lo crabito.
7. Como es la cabra, así será el cabrito.
8. Nola ahuntza hala pitika.

11.3 This exercise is intended to give you some idea how linguists work backwards to reconstruct the historical relations between languages. The data are taken from four modern dialects of Basque: Bizkaian (B), Gipuzkoan (G), Lapurdian (L) and Zuberoan (Z). In each case, the word in all four dialects is derived from the same ancestral form in an earlier (unattested) form of Basque. Can you work out what the ancestral form of each word must have been, and hence what changes must have occurred in each of the dialects?

In the special transcription used here, *s* and *S* represent two different kinds of s-sound, *r*, *rr* and *R* are three different kinds of r-sound, *g* always represents the sound in *give*, *zh* stands for the sound occurring in the middle of English *measure*, *a e i o u* are roughly as in Spanish or Italian, *ü* is roughly the vowel of French *tu*, *ñ* and *ll* represent two sounds not found in English, resembling the *ny* in *canyon* and the *lli* in *million*, and *x* is the sound in Scottish *loch* or German *ach*, while other symbols, including *j y sh ch*, have roughly their English values.

	B	**G**	**L**	**Z**
'bowel'	*eSte*	*eSte*	*heRtse*	*herrtse*
'bring'	*ekarri*	*ekarri*	*ekhaRi*	*ekharri*
'crazy'	*Soro*	*soro*	*soro*	*soo*
'daughter'	*alaba*	*alaba*	*alhaba*	*alhaba*
'donkey'	*aSto*	*aSto*	*aSto*	*aSto*
'eat'	*jan*	*xan*	*yan*	*zhan*
'fire'	*Su*	*Su*	*Su*	*Sü*
'five'	*boSt*	*boSt*	*boRts*	*borrts*
'gentleman'	*jaun*	*xaun*	*yaun*	*zhaün*
'head'	*buru*	*buru*	*buru*	*büü*
'hen'	*ollo*	*ollo*	*oilo*	*ollo*
'hit'	*jo*	*xo*	*yo*	*zho*
'house'	*eche*	*eche*	*eche*	*eche*
'long'	*luSe*	*luse*	*luse*	*lüse*
'moon'	*illarrgi*	*illarrgi*	*hilaRgi*	*hillarrgi*
'peach'	*mushika*	*mushika*	*mushika*	*müshika*
'proud'	*arro*	*arro*	*haRo*	*harro*
'stone'	*arri*	*arri*	*haRi*	*harri*

	B	**G**	**L**	**Z**
'ten'	*amarr*	*amarr*	*hamaR*	*hamarr*
'than'	*baño*	*baño*	*baino*	*baño*
'wheat'	*gari*	*gari*	*gari*	*gai*
'window'	*leio*	*leio*	*leiho*	*leiho*
'you'	*Su*	*su*	*su*	*sü*

Here's an example of how to go about this exercise. Consider the r-sounds. First, we note the following correspondence (∅ = zero):

    B *r* : G *r* : L *r* : Z ∅   e.g., 'crazy'

So let's assume that earlier Basque had *r* in these words, and that Z has lost it, while the other dialects have retained it. Now we note further:

    B *rr* : G *rr* : L *R* : Z *rr*   e.g., 'bring'

It seems reasonable to assume that earlier Basque had *rr* in these words, and that L has changed *rr* to *R*, while the other dialects have not changed this sound. Finally, we note a third correspondence:

    B ∅ : G ∅ : L *R* : Z *rr*   e.g., 'bowel'

This looks a bit like the second one, but this time B and G have zero instead of *rr*. However, observe that this third pattern only occurs as part of a larger correspondence:

    B *St* : G *St* : L *Rts* : Z *rrts*

Therefore, we can assume that these words too originally had *rr*, but that the sequence *rrts* has exceptionally changed into *St* in B and G.

11.4 Barry Fell, in his book *America B.C.*, argues that there was extensive contact between Europeans and North Americans long before the Viking voyages to North America. Among the evidence he cites are the following correspondences between Northeastern Algonkian, a group of languages spoken in parts of Canada and the United States, and the Celtic language Scots Gaelic:

Algonkian	**Gaelic**	**Meaning**
bhanem	*ban*	'woman'
alnoba	*allaban*	'person' (A), 'immigrant' (G)
lhab	*lion-obhair*	'netting'
odana	*dun*	'town'
na'lwiwi	*na h-uile*	'everywhere'
kladen	*claden*	'frost' (A), 'snowflake' (G)
pados	*bata*	'boat'
monaden	*monadh*	'mountain'
aden	*ard*	'height'
cuiche	*cuithe*	'gorge'

What conclusions, if any, may be drawn from these data? Do the data support Fell's hypothesis of prehistoric contact?

12 THE BIRTH AND DEATH OF LANGUAGES

> When two or more languages come into contact, it is possible for a new language to be born, or for some of the old languages to die out.

So far in this book we have looked at the way in which languages are derived from ancestral languages. We have seen that, with the passage of time, a single language tends to break up into what are at first distinct dialects and then ultimately different languages. In particular, we have seen how a single language, Proto-Indo-European, has, in the space of 6,000 years, fragmented into many dozens of modern languages, most of them so different from one another that it took decades of careful scholarly work to reveal their common ancestry.

Of course, PIE itself must have been descended from a still more remote ancestor spoken at an even earlier period, but the data and the methods at our disposal are not sufficient to trace the history of the Indo-European family back any further. It is possible, perhaps even probable, that some of the other language families we have identified share an exceedingly ancient common ancestor with the Indo-European languages, but at present we have no way of finding out.

Most of the 5,000 or so languages which are spoken today are derived in just such a way from a series of increasingly remote ancestors, stretching back in an unbroken line to the very beginnings of human speech. We have very little idea when our ancestors first began to speak: scholars variously estimate the time of the beginning of language at anywhere from 35,000 years ago to well over a million years ago, with a figure of around 120,000 years perhaps being the most popular guess. Whatever the correct figure, almost all modern languages are equally 'old', in that they can all trace their ancestry back to the beginning of speech in this way. Almost all – but there are some interesting exceptions.

In certain circumstances, it is possible for a new language to be born which is not descended from a single ancestor in the way I have already described. We now know that exactly this has happened on a number of occasions during historical times. It happens when speakers of different languages come into contact and need to have extensive dealings with one another. Consider, for example, the case of New Guinea.

Something like a thousand different languages are spoken on the large island of New Guinea: almost every valley has its own distinct language. For millennia, the inhabitants coped with this diversity simply by learning their neighbours' languages. Every New Guinean routinely learned to speak four or five languages while growing up: the language of the local community and the languages of the nearest neighbours. Such multilingualism was accepted as a normal part of everyone's life in a way that would stupefy a British school pupil struggling to get to grips with a single foreign language. When Europeans began to settle New Guinea in the eighteenth century, however, something else happened. Under urgent pressure to communicate, the European settlers and the original inhabitants began to piece together a kind of crude but serviceable linguistic system. Bits of grammar and vocabulary were taken from several local languages and from whichever European language was locally important: Dutch, English or German. The resulting system in each area was what we call a PIDGIN: a reduced language stitched together from bits and pieces of other languages, showing a good deal of variation, with a limited capacity for expression. These pidgins allowed people to communicate in a clumsy but effective way. **Pidgin**

As a result of the social and political changes introduced by the Europeans, New Guineans began to travel more widely than previously, and in some cases men and women married who had no language in common except the local pidgin. Naturally, they taught the pidgin to their children as a first language. This new generation of native pidgin speakers quickly began to turn their native tongue into a full-fledged language by creating new vocabulary and more elaborate grammatical structures. The result is no longer a pidgin: we call it a CREOLE. A creole is simply a former pidgin which has **Creole** become somebody's mother tongue and which has been enriched and elaborated to the point where it is just like any other language. The English-based creole of New Guinea now has a sizeable number of native speakers, and as a result a new language has come into existence within the last two centuries. This creole is called Tok Pisin (apparently from the English 'talk business'), and it is now the national language of Papua New Guinea.

Much the same thing has happened many times in other parts of the world. The Africans who were forcibly imported into the Caribbean by European slavers came from many different parts of Africa; they could originally speak neither to other Africans nor to the Europeans. Dozens of localized pidgins therefore sprang up; some of these eventually disappeared, as the children of the slaves learned the local European language, while others developed into creoles which are still spoken today. One of the most striking examples is Haitian Creole, derived originally from French and several African languages; this is now the mother tongue of the entire population of Haiti.

These modern creoles date only from the period of European expansion several centuries ago. It is, of course, quite possible that some other languages with a much longer history also started out as creoles thousands of years ago, but we shall probably never know for sure: once established, a creole is indistinguishable from any other language, and undergoes the same processes of linguistic change we have already examined.

So, most modern languages started out as dialects of much earlier languages, while some came about comparatively recently by the processes of pidginization and creolization. Now, if dialect splitting and creolization were the only things that ever happened to languages over time, the number of different languages would simply increase without limit. In fact, this has not happened. The estimated number of 5,000 languages spoken today is probably no greater than the number spoken, say, 2,000 years ago. And it is *certain* that fewer different languages are spoken today than were spoken 200 years ago. How can this be so?

It comes about because languages can and do die. At every point in human history, while some languages were gradually splitting into several distinct descendants, other languages were simply disappearing. Language death is a major feature of human history.

Language death

First, we must clarify what we mean by the DEATH OF A LANGUAGE, since the term 'dead language' is often used in a sense quite different from the one that is important here.

EXERCISE ✎

12.0 Latin, the language of the Roman Empire, is often called a 'dead' language, and it is true that there is no native speaker of Latin alive today who could converse with Julius Caesar if that famous soldier were somehow to be resurrected. (Some scholars and clerics have learned Latin as a second language, of course, but this is quite different from being a native speaker.) But, if Latin is dead, when, where and how did it die? If it didn't die, what happened to it instead? (Hint: if you find yourself puzzled by this, try asking yourself the same question about the Old English of King Alfred the Great.)

Discussion

Latin, in fact, has never 'died' – that is, there was never any time when people stopped speaking it. The language was spoken over most of the Roman Empire 2,000 years ago. But, with the passage of time, it has, of course, undergone the usual fate of a widespread language: it has broken up into several very different descendants.

With the political disintegration of the Roman Empire, there was no longer any unifying force sufficient to resist the natural tendency of the language to undergo different changes in different places, and so the spoken languages of widely separated parts of the old Empire have simply become more and more different from one another. In each generation, people learned the language from their parents and passed it on to their children, and there never were any last speakers of Latin. But the forms of Latin spoken today in Paris, Rome and Madrid (to take just three examples) are so different from the language of the Romans, and from one another, that we do not find it convenient to call them 'Latin' any longer: we prefer to call them 'French', 'Italian', 'Spanish', and so on, rather than 'Paris Latin', 'Rome Latin' and 'Madrid Latin'.

The case of Old English is similar, but not identical. Old English has gradually evolved into the dramatically different Modern English, but again there was no point at which people suddenly stopped speaking Old English and began to speak something else. Like Latin, Old English is therefore 'dead' only in that its modern forms are very different from it. Unlike the Latin case, though, we are happy to classify all the modern descendants of Old English as a single language, 'English', something we are reluctant to do with the modern forms of Latin.

In this unit, we are considering true language death: cases in which a language literally ceases to be spoken, and gives rise to no later forms at all. How can this happen?

One obvious way is for all the speakers of a language to die, without leaving any survivors. This might at first seem unlikely, but in fact it has happened a number of times, though perhaps not often naturally.

Between 1853 and 1870 the Yahi Indians of northern California were virtually exterminated – shot to death – by white settlers who coveted their land. Only sixteen Yahis survived the massacre; these fled into the wilderness, where they soon died of starvation, exposure and disease. All but one of them died without ever knowing a word of any language other than Yahi.

Much the same thing happened on a larger scale in Tasmania. Tasmania, a large island off the coast of Australia, had been inhabited for tens of thousands of years by people speaking perhaps two or three different languages. When British settlers arrived there in the early 1800s, they drove the Tasmanians off the land by force of arms: thousands were murdered in cold blood by settlers, and British soldiers were authorized to shoot Tasmanians on sight. By 1830 only 200 Tasmanians remained alive; these survivors were rounded up and placed in a kind of concentration camp, where most of them died.

Similar horror stories accompanied much of the European settlement of Australia, of North America and of South America, and possibly also the Bantu settlement of southern Africa and many other such large-scale movements of technologically superior peoples. But most language death, mercifully, does not take place in such ghastly circumstances.

Much more frequently, a language dies when its speakers give up speaking it in favour of some other language. This can happen when a language comes into contact with another language which is perceived as being more prestigious.

This has happened, for example, to a number of languages formerly spoken in the British Isles. Three centuries ago, apart from English, at least the following languages were spoken here: Welsh in most of Wales, Cornish (related to Welsh) in Cornwall, Gaelic in the Scottish Highlands, Irish in most of Ireland, Manx (related to Irish) in the Isle of Man, and Norn (a Scandinavian language) in the Orkneys and Shetlands; in addition, a variety of Norman French was spoken in the Channel Islands, and Romany (related to the languages of northern India) was spoken by Travellers ('Gysies') throughout the British Isles.

Since that time, all these languages have receded in the face of English, and some of them have disappeared entirely. Cornish was the first to go. On the one hand, Cornish speakers increasingly realized that a knowledge of English was a passport to success in the wider world of England; on the other, the use of Cornish was prohibited and suppressed by the English authorities, and Cornish protests were put down by force of arms. By the eighteenth century, knowledge of Cornish was confined to adults, and all the children in Cornwall spoke only English; Mrs Dolly Pentreath, who died in 1777, was possibly the last native speaker of Cornish, though some scholars believe a few others may have survived for another thirty years or so.

Orkney and Shetland Norn disappeared at around the same time. This Scandinavian language, introduced by Viking settlers nearly a thousand years earlier, succumbed to the increasing prestige of English in much the same way as Cornish.

Manx lasted rather longer in the face of English pressure. It is reported that Mr Ned Maddrell, who died in 1974 at the age of 97, was the last native speaker of Manx.

Romany has not quite died out, but it is still spoken only by a few Travellers in Wales. All Travellers in England and Ireland now speak English as their first language, though they retain a number of Romany words which they use among themselves as a kind of badge of identification.

Channel Islands French has not yet disappeared, but all speakers of the language are now middle-aged or elderly; no children speak it, and its death cannot be far away.

The position of Irish is not much better. Two centuries ago, Irish was spoken by a majority of the Irish population; today, in spite of vigorous efforts by the Irish government to preserve the language, Irish as a mother tongue is close to extinction. One recent study concludes that there are perhaps no more than 1,100 people in

Ireland who are genuinely more at home in Irish than in English, and all of these are eager for their children to learn English.

Scots Gaelic, once the first language throughout the Highlands, is now confined to the Western Isles and a few neighbouring parts of the mainland. There it is still the everyday language of perhaps 80,000 people, but virtually all of these are bilingual in English, and it is difficult to see a bright future for Gaelic.

Finally, Welsh has been the most resistant of all the minority languages of Britain. Once the language of the entire population of Wales (and, before the Anglo-Saxon invasion, of England), Welsh is now spoken by only 18 per cent of Welsh people, totalling about 600,000 speakers, and all of them are bilingual in English. Until recently, Welsh was subjected to much the same oppressive measures as Cornish: it was only a few years ago, for example, that schoolchildren in Wales were punished for speaking Welsh. Now there is extensive Welsh-language education and broadcasting, and the decline in the number of Welsh speakers has been halted, at least temporarily. But it may be too late: most Welsh speakers are keenly aware that a knowledge of Welsh confers opportunities only in Wales, while a knowledge of English confers opportunities throughout Britain and the world.

Throughout human history there have been innumerable such instances of people abandoning their language in favour of some other language seen as more prestigious or more useful. This happened to the very first language ever written down, Sumerian, the language of the land of Sumer in southern Mesopotamia between 5,000 and 6,000 years ago. After the Sumerians were conquered by their northern neighbours the Akkadians, they gradually abandoned their language in favour of Akkadian, a relative of Arabic and Hebrew which was unrelated to Sumerian, and the Sumerian language finally died out, much like Manx and Cornish millennia later.

Some 2,500 years ago, Latin was an insignificant language spoken by a small number of people in and around the city of Rome. But the Romans went on, first to overrun the peninsula of Italy, and then to carve out a huge empire all round the Mediterranean Sea. And they took their Latin language with them. By about AD 400 at the latest, not only in Italy, but also in what are now France, Spain and Portugal, Latin had completely displaced a wide range of previously spoken languages, all of which were abandoned by their speakers. The only exception to this obliteration of earlier languages is Basque. Spoken today by some 600,000 people at the western end of the Pyrenees, Basque has no living relatives, and it is the sole survivor of the ancient pre-Indo-European languages of western Europe.

In today's world, with its nation–states wielding strong centralized authority, with its rapid transport and communications, and with its influential mass media, languages are dying at a rate perhaps unprecedented in the history of human existence. Almost everywhere, in the face of a combination of pressures from the local prestige language, whole communities are abandoning their traditional languages. We can now see languages dying in front of our eyes.

A few years ago, Mrs Laura Fish Somersal of Alexander Valley, California, was found to be the sole surviving speaker of the North American language Wappo; Mrs Fish was already in her eighties, and, in 1992 she sadly died; Wappo has now joined Sumerian and Cornish in the ranks of dead languages. In 1970, the British linguist Bob Dixon succeeded in tracking down Mr Albert Bennett, the last surviving speaker of the Australian language Mbabaram; Mr Bennett died a few months later, and another language disappeared forever. The twentieth century has already seen perhaps more language deaths than any preceding century, but this dubious distinction will surely pass to the twenty-first century in its turn.

SUMMARY

- When speakers come into contact who have no language in common, the result may be the creation of a pidgin.
- If a pidgin is learned by children as their first language, it becomes a creole: a new natural language.
- Languages can and do die.
- This can happen because all the speakers of a language die without learning any other language.
- More usually, it happens when the speakers of a language gradually abandon it in favour of some other language.
- At present, languages are dying at a rate which is probably unprecedented.

EXERCISES

12.1 When a language is in the advanced stages of being replaced by another language, would you expect any changes in it? If so, what kinds of change?

12.2 After a language dies, is there any possibility that it can ever be brought back to life again? If so, can it once again become a mother tongue, or can it only be acquired as a second language?

12.3 In the text, I have rather oversimplified the linguistic picture of Britain. Apart from English, Welsh and Scots Gaelic, there are a number of other languages spoken by substantial numbers of people in Britain today. What are some of these other languages? Are they also dying, or is their position rather different?

12.4 On the whole, is it, in your view, a good thing or a bad thing that some languages die out in the face of competition from other more prestigious languages? In the British Isles, for example, is it good or bad that Cornish, Norn, Romany and Manx have disappeared, and that Irish and Scots Gaelic have nearly disappeared? Will it be a gain or a loss for the Welsh if Welsh too should disappear? Do you have the same or a different view about the loss of Australian languages like Mbabaram, Dyirbal and Gumbainggar in favour of English?

13 ATTITUDES TOWARDS LANGUAGE CHANGE

> Throughout history, older and more conservative speakers have objected to changes in the language whenever they have noticed them. These attitudes are still with us today, but they rarely have much effect on the development of the language.

Consider the following sentence:

Hopefully we'll arrive in time for lunch.

Do you regard this as perfectly normal English, or do you find it strange or worse? Do your friends agree with you? Your teachers?

In fact, the vast majority of English speakers, especially younger speakers, undoubtedly regard such sentences as perfectly normal and would not hesitate to use them in spontaneous conversation. But some English speakers take a very different view. The problem, for these other speakers, is the way in which the word *hopefully* is used in the above example. Until not so many years ago, it was simply impossible to use this word in the particular way illustrated above: an English speaker would have had to say something like *I hope we'll arrive in time for lunch*. But around 1970 this new use of *hopefully* began to occur in British English, after establishing itself a few years earlier in the United States. My example sentence therefore represents a change in English, an innovation which took place only about a quarter of a century ago. And this innovation has not been well received by everyone.

Here is what Mr Philip Howard, a well-known writer on language, has to say about this use of *hopefully*: he describes it as 'objectionable', 'ambiguous', 'obscure', 'ugly', 'aberrant', 'pretentious' and 'illiterate'; finally, playing his ace, he asserts that it was 'introduced by sloppy American academics'. In short, he doesn't seem to like it much.

Philip Howard is not alone in his dislike of this usage: many other writers have complained about it, often with similar bitterness. But why should a usage which seems so natural and unremarkable to most of the population attract such hostility from the rest?

The key point to notice here is that virtually all the English speakers who object to the new use of *hopefully* are middle-aged or older. That is, they are people who had already been using English for decades before this particular innovation occurred. Moreover, they are mostly also people who are especially well educated, and who take a particular interest in the use of language. Such people are often very conservative in their view of language; they are perhaps particularly inclined to view any changes in the English they grew up with as instances of 'sloppiness' or 'corruption'.

This hostility to language change is far from new. Recall that in **Unit 7** I pointed out that the new grammatical construction in *My house is being painted* was attacked in the eighteenth century as 'confusing', 'illogical', 'clumsy' and 'monstrous'. Indeed, around 2,000 years ago Roman writers were making hostile comments about some of the changes which were occurring in the spoken Latin of their day. At almost every time, and in almost every place, there appears to be a body of conservative opinion which holds that the language reached some kind of pinnacle of perfection a generation or so ago, and is now going rapidly downhill with all these 'ugly', 'sloppy', 'illiterate' new usages we keep hearing nowadays.

In most cases, this hostility to language change, however vigorous and articulate, has no lasting effect. The older speakers who object to the new forms simply die, leaving the field to the younger speakers who have grown up with them and who regard them as normal. As these younger speakers grow older, they will no doubt object in turn to the innovations favoured by the next generation, with the same result. However we may feel about the fact, resistance to language change is nearly always futile.

Of course, a certain amount of inertia in resisting language change is no bad thing. After all, we don't want the language to change so fast that children cannot talk to their grandparents, or so fast that no one can read anything written a hundred years earlier. Language changes quite fast enough as it is. We have great difficulty in reading what our ancestors wrote 400 years ago, and doubtless our descendants 400 years from now will find it at least equally difficult to read what we are writing now, or to understand the tape recordings and films that we will bequeath them.

EXERCISE

13.0 Here are a few examples of contemporary English usage which many conservative speakers vigorously object to. In each case, do you find the example normal and unremarkable, or do you too object to it? If you find it normal, can you put your finger on the problem perceived by the conservatives?

(a) This project was carried out by Sarah and myself.
(b) I tried to persuade Juliet to join the choir, but she was disinterested.
(c) Your analysis is questionable, but your data is certainly interesting.
(d) Just between you and I, Alison and Steve have broken up.
(e) The audience were literally glued to their seats.
(f) We expect the contract to be finalized on Tuesday.
(g) She was undaunted by the enormity of the task in front of her.
(h) Senna is one of those drivers who always seems to get the best out of his car.
(i) Having said that, there's no reason we shouldn't do better next week.
(j) Somebody has forgotten their umbrella.

Discussion

Here are the forms preferred by conservative users of English:

(a) ... by Sarah and me (*myself* can only follow *I*)
(b) ... she was uninterested (*disinterested* means 'having nothing to gain or lose', not 'apathetic')
(c) ... your data are interesting (*data* is a plural form)
(d) ... between you and me (*I* cannot occur after a preposition)
(e) ... were glued (*literally* means 'actually')
(f) ... to be completed on Tuesday (*finalize* is not recognized as a real word)
(g) ... by the magnitude of the task (*enormity* means 'terrible crime', not 'large size')
(h) ... of those drivers who always seem (*seem* must agree with *drivers*, not with *one*)
(i) various other forms possible, but *having said that*, if used, must be immediately followed by I
(j) ... his umbrella or ... his or her umbrella (*somebody* must take a singular form like *his*, not a plural one like *their*)

We have been speaking of hostility to innovations in language, but there is another kind of attitude that deserves some attention: some people *want* to see changes which have not yet occurred. One of the most striking contemporary illustrations of this is the view of feminists who object to what they see as the built-in sexism of English and other languages.

One of the most obvious examples of such sexism in English is the use of *man* to mean not only 'male person' but also 'human being(s)', in locutions like *Men first reached the Americas 11,000 years ago* and *Man has a larger brain than any ape*. Many women understandably object to such usages, and have campaigned to have them replaced by other, non-sexist, forms.

More difficult is the existence of utterances like *Somebody has forgotten his umbrella*, where male *his* is used even though the sex of the owner is unspecified. Here *his or her umbrella* would be unappealingly clumsy, and English speakers are increasingly solving the problem by resorting to *Somebody has forgotten their umbrella*, which neatly avoids any charge of sexism but attracts the ire of conservatives, who regard it as 'illogical'. And even this neat-looking solution runs into difficulties in cases like *When a person doesn't know what to do with themselves...*, which sounds bizarre to many people.

Still other difficulties arise with words like *chairman, postman, freshman, spokesman, statesman, fireman* and *anchorman*, all denoting positions which are frequently filled by women. And yet graver difficulties are presented by such established words as *manslaughter, manpower, man-hour, man-made, manhole* and *man-eating (shark)*, not to mention the phrase *to man (a position)*. Even if we agree that the elimination of such sexist forms is desirable (and not everyone does agree), it is often far from clear what we can do about them.

SUMMARY

- Older speakers frequently object vigorously to recent changes in the language, regarding the new forms as 'sloppy', 'illogical' or 'illiterate'.
- This reaction is not new, but has been with us for many centuries.
- Such objections rarely have any effect on the language.
- Some speakers, in contrast, may object to long-established forms and usages and campaign for changes which have not yet occurred.

EXERCISES

13.1 Language can be manipulated, either unconsciously or purposefully, to express particular attitudes embraced by the user; sometimes this involves the deliberate creation of new forms. Here are some examples, all of them adapted from actual newspaper reports, books or advertisements. In each case, what attitude is the writer expressing? How might the example be differently expressed to expose the attitude in question?

(a) The American pioneers trekked across the prairies with their seed corn, their livestock and their wives.

(b) General Dreedle admitted that the airstrike had inflicted significant collateral damage.
(c) We can arrange a complete memorial service for your loved one.
(d) The recent increase in house repossessions is disappointing.
(e) He went berserk and attacked his next-door neighbour's wife.
(f) We propose a rationalization of staffing levels.
(g) Here is a new fantasy epic in the great tradition of *The Lord of the Rings*.

13.2 Basque is chiefly spoken in northern Spain. Below is a list of some Spanish words, followed in each case by the word used for the same meaning by most older Basque speakers, and then the word used by many younger Basque speakers. What seems to have happened earlier in Basque? What seems to be happening now? What kind of attitude is being exhibited by Basque speakers?

Meaning	Spanish	Older Basque	Younger Basque
'accordion'	*acordeón*	*akordeoi*	*eskusoinu*
'airplane'	*avión*	*abioi*	*hegazkin*
'bra'	*sostén*	*sosten*	*bularretako*
'compass'	*brújula*	*bruxula*	*iparrorratz*
'custom'	*costumbre*	*kostunbre*	*ohitura*
'nurse'	*enfermera*	*enfermera*	*erizain*
'photograph'	*foto*	*foto*	*argazki*
'police'	*policia*	*polizia*	*ertzain*
'refrigerator'	*frigorífico*	*frigorifiko*	*hozkailu*
'student'	*estudiante*	*estudiante*	*ikasle*
'triangle'	*triángulo*	*triangulo*	*hiruki*
'umbrella'	*paraguas*	*parauas*	*euritako*
'Vittoria' (town name)	*Vitoria*	*Bitoria*	*Gasteiz*

13.3 Another type of change in English which has not yet occurred but which many people have been arguing for is a rationalization of our complex spelling system, both to make our spelling more regular and to bring it closer to the pronunciation. How do you feel about such a proposal? Here is one possibility for a regularized spelling system; it is a rewriting of the first sentence of this paragraph:

Unudhur tiyp ov chaynj in Ingglish wich haz not yet ukurd but wich meni peepul hav been argyuing for iz u rashunuliyzayshun ov aur kompleks speling sistum, boeth tuu mayk aur speling mor regyulur and tuu bring it kloesur tuu dhu prununsiayshun.

A new spelling system along these lines would undoubtedly be very much easier for children to learn. But can you think of any possible objections to such a reform of our spelling? (Hint: have another look at **Unit 5**.)

13.4 Have another look at the new words listed in **Exercise 1.1** in **Unit 1**. Are there any words in the list that you object to? If so, why do you object? Do you find some of the words ugly, or silly, or unnecessary, or what? Do your parents or other people have different views?

---

14 PUTTING IT ALL TOGETHER

The central theme of this book is that language is always changing. In vocabulary, in pronunciation, in grammar, in meaning, and to some extent in spelling, change is a constant and unavoidable fact of life. Language has been changing since it first appeared on earth; it is changing now; it will surely continue to change for as long as human beings survive.

Moreover, a single language does not change everywhere in the same way. When a language is spoken over any significant stretch of territory, changes which occur in one area do not necessarily spread to other areas. As a result, with the passage of time, differences slowly but steadily accumulate among the regional varieties of the language. For a while we can regard these regional varieties as merely dialects of a single language, but eventually the differences become so great that we are forced to regard the varieties as entirely distinct languages. These new languages in turn, if they survive, will inevitably undergo the same processes and gradually split further into new dialects and eventually into further new languages.

Very often older speakers will object strongly to changes when they notice them, but this rarely has much effect. Sooner or later the older speakers die, taking their objections with them, and their place is taken by a younger generation which has grown up with the new forms and regards them as normal. Language change is remorseless.

For tens of thousands of years, languages have been splitting into dialects and then new languages, again and again and again. Very often people have migrated to new territories, taking their language with them, and accelerating the process of linguistic divergence by doing so.

Inevitably, speakers of some languages come into contact with speakers of other languages. Such contact can have important consequences, particularly when one language is perceived by its speakers as being less prestigious than a neighbouring language. One language may borrow large numbers of words from its neighbour; it may even borrow pronunciations and grammatical forms. In the extreme case, a language may be entirely abandoned by its speakers in favour of another, and become a dead language. Uncountably many languages have died in this manner over the ages, while some others have been literally murdered in the slaughter of their speakers by more powerful neighbours.

At present, thanks to the existence of strong, centralized nation-states and of efficient transport and communications, languages are dying at a rate perhaps unprecedented in human history, and the number of different languages spoken on the planet is dropping rapidly.

On the other hand, contact can occasionally, when conditions are favourable, result in the creation of brand-new languages by the process of pidgin formation followed by creolization. Very many pidgins and creoles were formed during the age of European expansion several centuries ago; some of these still survive today, though it is unlikely that many new ones are being created now.

To some extent, linguists can work backwards to establish the history of large numbers of languages. They can often identify languages which are 'genetically related', that is, which have sprung from a single common ancestor. Dozens of language families have been identified in this way.

In particular, we now know a great deal about the origin and history of English. Around 6,000 years ago, probably somewhere in eastern Europe, an unidentified people were speaking an unrecorded language which we call Proto-Indo-European, or PIE. The speakers of PIE gradually spread out over an enormous area of Europe and Asia, and during the succeeding millennia PIE, like all languages, repeatedly split into generations of new languages. Many of these languages displaced the earlier languages of Europe, most of which disappeared as a result. One particular group of people carried a descendant of PIE into Scandinavia in the first millennium BC; we call their unrecorded language Proto-Germanic. The speakers of Proto-Germanic slowly spread out over much of Europe, especially northern Europe, and by AD 500 or so the closely related Germanic dialects which we call 'Ingvaeonic' were being spoken on the east coast of the North Sea.

At about this time some of these people migrated to Britain, taking their language with them; separated from its continental cousins, this British variety of Ingvaeonic developed into the language we call English. The conquest of England by the French-speaking Normans in 1066 submerged English only temporarily; within a few generations it had re-emerged, greatly changed in its grammar and stuffed with words borrowed from French, to become in turn the national language of England, the language of the British Empire, and finally the most widely used language in the world. In the process it has largely extinguished, through a mixture of persuasion and violence, the other languages of the British Isles and the indigenous languages of North America and Australia.

The worldwide spread of English is unprecedented in the whole history of human languages. Only time will tell whether our technological advances will allow us to maintain a more or less unified form of English across the globe, or whether, like Proto-Indo-European before it, English will gradually succumb to the combination of remorseless change and geographical separation, and break up into a new family of daughter languages.

FURTHER READING

If you'd like to read more about language change, an excellent place to start would be

> Jean Aitchison, *Language Change: Progress or Decay?*, 2nd edn, Cambridge: Cambridge University Press, 1991.

This is a very readable introductory book which has a lot to say about the way in which innovations spread through speech communities, an aspect rather neglected in this workbook.

There are a number of more substantial university-level textbooks of language change; among the better ones are

> Terry Crowley, *An Introduction to Historical Linguistics*, 2nd edn, Oxford: Oxford University Press, 1992.
>
> Winfred P. Lehmann, *Historical Linguistics*, 3rd edn, London: Routledge, 1992.

To find out more about English, you might start with

> David Crystal, *The English Language*, London: Penguin, 1988.

This is a fascinating little book covering everything from truckers' jargon to Melanesian Pidgin English, from obscure Scrabble® words to American place names, but it also includes a brief history of English. More substantial, but still very readable, is

> Robert McCrum, William Cran and Robert MacNeil, *The Story of English*, 2nd edn, London: Faber & Faber/BBC Books, 1992.

This work is especially good on the social history of English – that is, the way the history of the language relates to the history of the English-speaking peoples.

Finally, there are several still more substantial histories of English which are aimed mainly at university students:

> Albert C. Baugh and Thomas Cable, *A History of the English Language*, 4th edn, London: Routledge, 1993.
>
> Thomas Pyles, *The Origins and Development of the English Language*, 2nd edn, New York: Harcourt, Brace, Jovanovich, 1971.
>
> Barbara Strang, *A History of English*, London: Methuen, 1970.
>
> Joseph M. Williams, *Origins of the English Language: A Social and Linguistic History*, London: Collier Macmillan, 1975.

Note that the book by Barbara Strang runs backwards; that is, it starts with the present and works back to the earliest days of English.

You can find a vast number of books on the histories of English words, ranging from the light-hearted to the scholarly. A light-hearted one is

> Martin Manser, *The Guinness Book of Words*, Enfield, Middx: Guinness Books, 1988.

A little dryer, but much more detailed, is

> J. A. Sheard, *The Words of English*, New York: W. W. Norton, 1966.

Pronunciation is not an easy subject to read about unless you have some grounding in phonetics (the study of speech sounds). But several of the books mentioned above have sections on the history of English pronunciation, and the following book includes a vast amount of information about the pronunciation of English all over Britain and the world:

> J. C. Wells, *Accents of English*, 3 vols, Cambridge: Cambridge University Press, 1982.

For most other aspects of the history of English, it is necessary to turn to the textbooks mentioned above.

There are several very readable books on the dialects of English spoken in Britain and around the world:

> John Platt, Heidi Weber and Ho Min Lian, *The New Englishes*, London: Routledge, 1984.
>
> Peter Trudgill, *The Dialects of England*, Oxford: Blackwell, 1990.
>
> Peter Trudgill and Jean Hannah, *International English: A Guide to Varieties of Standard English*, 2nd edn, London: Edward Arnold, 1985.
>
> Peter Trudgill and Arthur Hughes, *English Accents and Dialects*, London: Edward Arnold, 1987.

The first of these concentrates particularly on the varieties of English spoken in Africa, Asia and the Caribbean.

A survey of Indo-European and the other major language families is given in Part 9 of

> David Crystal, *The Cambridge Encyclopedia of Language*,

Cambridge: Cambridge University Press, 1987.

Similar summaries are given in very many popular books on language of the sort you can probably find in your local library. A more substantial, but still readable, account of Indo-European is given in

> W. B. Lockwood, *Indo-European Philology*, London: Hutchinson, 1969.

A survey of more than a hundred Indo-European languages is provided in

> W. B. Lockwood, *A Panorama of the Indo-European Languages*, London: Hutchinson, 1972.

Language birth and death are well covered in the Jean Aitchison book mentioned above. The extermination of the Yahi and of the Tasmanians is described in

> Jared Diamond, *The Rise and Fall of the Third Chimpanzee*, London: Vintage, 1991.

Most of this fascinating book is not about language at all, but about human behaviour. The story of Bob Dixon and Albert Bennett is told in

> R. M. W. Dixon, *Searching for Aboriginal Languages: Memoirs of a Field Worker*, Chicago: University of Chicago Press, 1984.

A very readable book on attitudes to language change is

> Lars Andersson and Peter Trudgill, *Bad Language*, Oxford: Blackwell, 1990.

The quotation from Philip Howard is taken from

> Philip Howard, *New Words for Old*, London: Hamish Hamilton, 1977.

A good library will, however, provide a number of books by Mr Howard and by other writers expressing comparable hostility to recent innovations.

There is a vast literature on sexist language; two accessible books are

> Deborah Cameron, *Feminism and Linguistic Theory*, London: Macmillan, 1985.
> David Graddol and Joan Swann, *Gender Voices*, Oxford: Blackwell, 1989.

But perhaps the most stunning piece ever written on the deep-seated sexism of English is

> Douglas R. Hofstadter, 'A person paper on purity in language', in Douglas R. Hofstadter, *Metamagical Themas: Questing for the Essence of Mind and Pattern*, Harmondsworth: Viking Penguin, 1985, pp. 159–67.

The curious thing about this article is not that it was written by a man, but that it never mentions sexism at all.

FURTHER EXERCISES

Here are some suggestions for further exercises, mostly in the form of small projects, which you might like to try in order to broaden your understanding of some of the topics discussed in this workbook.

1 Choose two or three passages, each of a hundred words or so, from sources which are as different as possible – say, a tabloid newspaper and a chemistry textbook. For each passage, look up the origin of each word in a dictionary that provides this information. You might like to use the following categories to organize your findings:

  (a) native English;
  (b) Old Norse;
  (c) Latin;
  (d) Greek;
  (e) French;
  (f) all other languages.

It's a good idea to count a particular word only once, no matter how often it occurs in the passage; otherwise, the very common native words like *the* and *of* will dominate your figures. How do the figures compare for your different passages? What conclusions can you draw about the way in which these different source languages have influenced the English vocabulary?

2 Try watching a television programme made in another part of the English-speaking world. If you're British, for example, try an American or an Australian programme. Try to take notes on any words, expressions, grammatical forms and (if possible) pronunciations which you wouldn't use yourself. Try looking up the words in a dictionary to see if they're labelled 'American' or 'Australian' or whatever.

3 Choose a scene from one of Shakespeare's plays and pick out the words and the grammatical forms you find there which would be abnormal or impossible in modern English. Most published versions of Shakespeare today use modernized spelling, so you probably won't be able to do the same with Shakespeare's spellings. Are any of the things you find so strange that you can't understand them without help?

4 Apart from the ones mentioned in this book, are there any words, forms or expressions people are using now which you are sure did not

exist a few years ago? Try keeping your eyes and ears open for a week to see if you can spot any new words or forms. If you find any, try to explain where they've come from or how they've been formed.

5   Possibly you don't speak English at home – perhaps, for example, you speak Bengali or Cantonese or Greek with your family. If so, do you notice any differences between the way you speak the language and the way it is spoken by your parents or grandparents or other members of the older generation? Can you see any evidence that your speech is more influenced by English than is your parents' speech? Even if you do speak English at home, perhaps you can still notice some differences between your speech and that of your parents.

APPENDIX

This appendix contains a number of English words which occur in the exercises in the book, together with various types of information about those words that may prove useful in tackling the exercises. Not all the words from the exercises are included here, but enough of them are to give you some useful assistance with most of the exercises. Also included are some Greek and Latin elements used in forming English words.

al a Middle English form of *all* or of *although*.

amphi- 'both' (from Greek).

'appen a word meaning 'apparently', 'probably' or 'possibly', typical of Derbyshire and much of the north of England.

arrive originally, 'reach a river bank'.

atmo- 'breath' (from Greek).

banana from a West African language.

basho a sumo wrestling tournament (from Japanese).

Betweensea Eyots Paul Jennings' term for the *Channel Islands*.

bi- 'life', 'living' (from Greek).

bibli- 'book' (from Greek).

board the side of a ship.

bonzer 'excellent'; a typical Australian word.

book beech bark was once used for writing.

boon originally, 'prayer'.

brandy from Dutch *brandewijn* 'burnt wine'.

burn a Scottish form of *bourne* 'stream', as in *Bournemouth*.

butter from Ancient Greek.

bylle an obsolete spelling of *bill*, which once meant 'letter', 'note'.

call someone's bluff an expression from poker.

candidate originally, 'dressed in white clothing'.

chapel the cloak of St Martin of Tours, an important religious relic, was once kept in a chapel.

chipmunk a small ground squirrel (from an Algonkian language).

chocolate from Nahuatl.

cinnamon from Hebrew.

clue originally, a ball of yarn.

cockpit originally, a pit in which cockfights were held.

comon an old spelling of *common*, which could once be a verb meaning 'discuss'.

cultur- 'growing' (from Latin).

daytimer an afternoon disco.

dendro- 'tree' (from Greek).

derm- 'skin' (from Greek).

devil to pay *pay* formerly meant 'to caulk (a seam) with pitch', and the *devil* was a particularly difficult seam to caulk.

diesel from the name of the inventor, *Rudolf Diesel*.

diffuser an attachment for a hair dryer.

dino- 'terrible' (from Greek).

dishevelled originally, 'with hair disarranged'.

doldrums an area of the sea where no wind blows and sailing ships are unable to make headway.

doner (kebab) from Turkish *döner* 'turning'.

duppy 'ghost'; a common word in the West Indies.

dweeb a tiresome or foolish person (from American English).

dynam- 'movement' (from Greek).

electron from the Greek for 'amber'; electricity was first noticed when people rubbed amber with fur.

escape originally, 'take off one's cloak'.

fee originally, 'livestock'.

feyne a Middle English spelling of *feign* 'pretend'.

frock originally, a monk's costume.

geeky boring, tiresome.

glot- 'tongue', 'language' (from Greek).

goulash from Hungarian.

helico- 'screw' (from Greek).

hir an ancient word for *their*, now obsolete.

hydro- 'water' (from Greek).

hypo- 'under' (from Greek).

jib the small triangular sail at the front of a sailing ship, the first part you see as the ship approaches you.

ketchup from Chinese.

lemon from Arabic.

leotard from *Jules Léotard*, a French aerialist who popularized the garment.

lewd originally, 'clumsy', 'unsophisticated'.

limerick from *Limerick*, a place in Ireland.

lingu- 'tongue', 'language' (from Latin).

log- 'word'; by extension, 'study' (from Greek).

lyhe an eccentric spelling of *like*, which originally meant 'please'.

manufacture originally, 'make by hand'.

marin- 'sea' (from Latin).

mediocre originally, 'halfway up the mountain'.

metr- 'measure' (from Greek).

micro- 'small' (from Greek).

Middlesea Paul Jennings' term for the *Mediterranean*.

miniature originally, 'coloured red'.

money the Roman goddess Juno was nicknamed *Moneta*, 'the admonisher', and her temple in Rome was used for minting coins.

moote a Middle English form of *must*.

multi- 'many' (from Latin).

mustard from medieval French.

ny an old spelling of *nigh* 'near'.

orange from Persian.

overthingsome Paul Jennings' term for *metaphysical*.

phil- 'love' (from Greek).

phoenix from Ancient Greek.

phone 'sound', 'voice' (from Greek).

poise originally, 'weight'.

poly- 'many' (from Greek).

port from Portuguese *Oporto*, a city name.

potato from Taino, an extinct Caribbean language.

prove originally, 'test'.

pseud- 'false' (from Greek).

psych- 'soul', 'spirit' (from Greek).

pter- 'wing' (from Greek).

quarantine originally, 'confine for forty days'.

rhodo- 'rose' (from Greek).

ringpath Paul Jennings' term for *orbit*.

riposte an expression from fencing.

sack originally, a type of strong wine.

saur- 'lizard' (from Greek).

sci- 'know' (from Latin).

scrooge from *Ebenezer Scrooge*, a character in Dickens.

scrum pox a certain disease of rugby players.

sect- 'cut' (from Latin).

selfthrough Paul Jennings' term for *uncontaminated*.

September the year formerly began in March, not January.

shambles originally, 'butcher's slab'.

sherry from Spanish *jerez*, from the name of the region where sherry is produced.

silly originally, 'helpless'.

skill originally, 'understanding'.

skirt from Old Norse, and originally the same word as English *shirt*.

skorts short culottes (*skirt* plus *shorts*).

smeech 'smoke', 'smell' a West Country word.

son- 'sound' (from Latin).

strong suit an expression from bridge (the card game).

stymied an obsolete expression from golf.

sub- 'under' (from Latin).

switchmeangroup Paul Jennings' term for *metaphor*.

tele- 'far' (from Greek).

thermo- 'hot', 'heat' (from Greek).

thrown for a loss an expression from American football.

tiffin lunch (an old word which has dropped out of use in Britain but is still in use in India).

trans- 'across' (from Latin).

trypieceman Paul Jennings' term for *essayist*.

ultra- 'beyond' (from Latin).

unco a Scots word for 'strange', related to *uncouth*.

unthingsome Paul Jennings' term for *abstract*.

vandal from *Vandals*, an ancient barbarian tribe.

vest- 'dress' (from Latin).

viti- 'grapevine' (from Latin).

vivi- 'living' (from Latin).

wa a form of *we*, typical of Lincolnshire.

wade originally, 'go'.

washcloth a face flannel (the American word, of obvious formation).

window from Old Norse *vindauga* 'wind-eye'.

wine from Latin.

withtaking Paul Jennings' term for *concept*.

zo a Devonshire form of *so*, typical of much of the West Country.

INDEX

A reference to the form **8**:0 indicates page 0 in Unit 8. One of the form **Ex.** 10.3 indicates Exercise 10. 3 in Unit 10. And one of the form **Un.** 12 indicates that the term is discussed at length in Unit 12.

accents: **5**:25
acronyms: **4**:22
active: **7**:38
African languages: **Ex.** 1.4, **Ex.** 3.4, **11**:61, **12**:66
Afrikaans: **Ex.** 1.4; **10**:52
Afro-Asiatic languages: **11**:61
Akkadian: **12**:69
Albanian: **11**:60
Algonkian languages: **11**:61, **Ex.** 11.4
American English: **1**:2–3, **Ex.** 1.2, **3**:12, **5**:26, **Ex.** 7.1, **7**:36, **9**:48–9, **Ex.** 9.2
American Indian languages: **Ex.** 1.2, 3.12, **Ex.** 3.4, **12**:67
Anglo-Saxon: *see* Old English
Anglo-Saxon Chronicle: **2**:9
Arabic: **3**:13–14, **Ex.** 3.4, **11**:61
Armenian: **11**:60
attitudes to language change: **Ex.** 7.3, **Un.** 13
Austen, Jane: **8**:42
Australia: **5**:26, **9**:47
Australian languages: **3**:14, **11**:61, **12**:67, **12**:70, **Ex.** 12.4
Austronesian languages: **11**:61
Aztec: **Ex.** 3.4

back-formation: **4**:22
Basque: **Ex.** 11.2, **Ex.** 11.3, **12**:69, **Ex.** 13.2
Bennett, Albert: **12**:70
birth of languages: **Un.** 12

blending: **4**:22
borrowing: **Un.** 3, **Ex.** 4.4, **14**:79
Burmese: **11**:61

Canada: **5**:26–8
Catalan: **11**:59
Celtic languages: **11**:60, **Ex.** 11.4, **12**:70
Chaucer, Geoffrey: **2**.8, **Ex.** 2.3, **8**:41
Chinese: **3**:14, **Ex.** 3.4, **11**:61
clipping: **4**:21–2
compounding: **4**:19
contact: **Un.** 3, **14**:78–9
Cornish: **12**:68, **Ex.** 12.4
Creoles: **12**:65–6, **12**:70, **14**:79

Danish: **10**:51–2, **11**:58
death of languages: **Un.** 12, **14**:79
derivation: **4**:20–1
dialects: **1**:3, **Ex.** 1.4, **Un.** 9, **Ex.** 11.2, **14**:78
dictionaries: **6**:34
Dixon, Bob: **12**:70
Dutch: **3**:14, **Ex.** 3.4, **10**:51–2, **Ex.** 10.3, **11**:58

Early Modern English: **2**:8
East Anglia: **5**:27
Egyptian: **11**:61
Eskimo: **3**:13
Estonian: **11**:61
Ethiopia: **3**:13
euphemisms: **8**:42, **Ex.** 8.0

family of languages: **10**:52
Faroese: **10**:52
Fell, Barry: **Ex.** 11.4
Finnish: **3**:14, **11**:61
Fish Somersal, Laura: **12**:70
French: **1**:2–3, **Ex.** 1.3, **3**:14–15, **Ex.** 3.4, **6**:33, **11**:59, **12**:67–8, **14**:79
Frisian: **10**:51–2
Friulian: **11**:59

Gaelic: **3**:12–13, **Ex.** 11.4, **12**:69, **Ex.** 12.3, **Ex.** 12.4
Galician: **11**:59
genetic relations: **Un.** 10
generalization of meaning: **8**:42
Ge-Pano-Carib languages: **11**:61
German: **3**:14–15, **Ex.** 3.4, **7**:38, **10**:51–3, **10**:55, **Ex.** 10.0, **Ex.** 10.1, **Ex.** 10.2, **Ex.** 10.3, **11**:58–9
Germanic languages: **10**:53, **10**:55–6, **11**:60
Gothic: **10**:52, **10**:53–4
grammar, changes in: **Un.** 7
Greek: **3**:14, **Ex.** 3.2, **Ex.** 3.4, **4**:20, **Ex.** 8.2, **11**:60
Gujerati: **11**:60

Haitian Creole: **12**:66
Hausa: **11**:61
Hawaiian: **3**:14
Hindi: **3**:14, **Ex.** 3.4, **11**:60
Howard, Philip: **13**:72–3
Hungarian: **3**:14, **Ex.** 3.4, **11**:61

Icelandic: **10**:52
Indian languages: **11**:60, **12**:68
Indo-European languages: **11**:60, **14**:79
Ingvaeonic: **10**:52–3, **14**:79
Iranian languages: **11**:60
Ireland: **5**:25–7
Irish: **11**:60, **Ex.** 12.4
Italian: **3**:13, **3**:15, **Ex.** 3.3, **Ex.** 3.4, **11**:59, **12**:67

Japanese: **3**:13–15, **Ex.** 3.1, **Ex.** 3.3, **Ex.** 3.4
Johnson, Samuel: **6**:34

Kurdish: **11**:60
Kurgan: **11**:60

Lappish: **11**:61
Latin: **3**:14, **Ex.** 3.2, **Ex.** 3.4, **4**:20, **6**:33, **7**:38, **11**:60, **12**:69, **12**:73, **Ex.** 12.0
Lithuanian: **11**:60
long sounds: **5**:29

Longman Register of New Words: **1**:4

Maddrell, Ned: **12**:68
Manx: **12**:68, **Ex.** 12.4
Mbabaram: **12**:70
meaning, changes in: **Un.** 8
metaphor: **Ex.** 8.3
Middle English: **2**:9, **Ex.** 2.4
Midlands: **5**:26, **7**:36
Modern English: **Ex.** 2.4

Nahuatl: **Ex.** 3.4
New England: **1**:3
New Guinea: **12**:65
New Zealand: **5**:26, **5**:28
Niger–Congo languages: **11**:61
Norn: **12**:68, **Ex.** 12.4
Norwegian: **3**:14, **10**:52

Occitan: **11**:59
Old English: **2**:9–10, **Ex.** 4.0, **6**:32, **Ex.** 6.0, **Ex.** 7.0, **9**:47, **10**:54, **Ex.** 10.3, **Ex.** 12.0
Old High German: **10**:54
Old Icelandic: **10**:54
Old Norse: **Ex.** 3.3
Old Saxon: **10**:54
origin of language: **12**:64

passive: **7**:38–9
Paston Letters: **Ex.** 2.4
Pennsylvania, Western: **1**:3, **7**:36
Pentreath, Dolly: **12**:68
Persian: **3**:14, **Ex.** 3.4, **11**:60
pidgins: **12**:65, **12**:70, **14**:79
PIE: *see* Proto-Indo-European
pilgrims: **1**:2
plural: **Ex.** 1.2
Polish: **11**:60
Portuguese: **3**:14, **Ex.** 3.4, **11**:59
prefixation: **4**:21
pronunciation: **Un.** 5
Proto-Germanic: **10**:53–4, **11**:59–60, **14**:79
Proto-Indo-European: **11**:60, **12**:64, **14**:79
Proto-Romance: **11**:59

received pronunciation (RP): **5**:28
rhotic accents: **5**:26
Romance languages: **11**:59, **Ex.** 11.2
Romansh: **11**:59
Romany: **12**:68, **Ex.** 12.4
Rumanian: **Ex.** 3.4, **11**:59
Russian: **Ex.** 3.4, **7**:38, **11**:60

Sardinian: **11**:59
Scandinavian languages: **Ex.** 3.3, **12**:68

Scotland: **1**:3, **3**:12, **5**:26–8, **7**:36, **9**:47
Serbo-Croatian: **11**:60
sexism in language: **12**:74–5
Shakespeare, William: **2**:7, **Ex.** 2.1, **Ex.** 6.2, **Ex.** 7.4
short sounds: **5**:29
Siberian languages: **11**:61
singular: **Ex.** 7.2
Sino-Tibetan languages: **11**:61
Slavic languages: **11**:60
South Africa: **Ex.** 1.4, **5**:26, **10**:52
Spanish: **3**:13, **3**:15, **Ex.** 3.4, **11**:58–9, **Ex.** 11.0, **12**:67, **Ex.** 13.2
specialization of meaning: **8**:42
spelling: **Un.** 6, **Ex.** 13.3
suffixation: **4**:20–1
Sumerian: **12**:69
Swedish: **10**:52, **10**:55, **11**:59
systematic correspondence: **10**:53

Tamil: **Ex.** 3.4

Tasmanian languages: **12**:67
Thai: **11**:61
Tibetan: **11**:61
Turkish: **3**:13, **Ex.** 3.4

Ulster: **1**:3
Uralic languages: **11**:61
Urdu: **3**:14, **11**:60

Wales: **5**:26, **5**:28, **12**:69
Wappo: **12**:70
Webster, Noah: **6**:34
Welsh: **11**:60, **12**:69, **Ex.** 12.4
West Country: **5**:26, **7**:36
word-formation: **Un.** 4

Xhosa: **Ex.** 1.4

Yahi Indians: **12**:67
Yiddish: **Ex.** 3.3, **10**:52

Zulu: **Ex.** 1.4

注釈

p.VII USING THIS BOOK

1　　As the title suggests, this is a workbook on language change. It is not a textbook, and it is not designed to present you with a vast amount of information: other books are available if you would like to read further on the topic.

　ここに書かれているように、*Language Change* はワークブックである。EXERCISE を省略して全体を通読するだけでも、英語の歴史や言語変化を概観するのに適切な入門書となっているが、著者の R. L. Trask は、あくまで本書をワークのための手がかりとして利用してもらい、言語変化を「体感」してもらいたいと考えて本書を著したはずである。本書を能動的に使用しながら、英語の歴史についての理解を深めて欲しい。

p.1　Unit 1．LANGUAGE IS ALWAYS CHANGING

1　　Every language that people use changes constantly. English, for example, has been changing throughout its history and it is still changing today.

　言語が変化するということは、本書の中心的なテーマである。このユニットでは、いくつかの具体例を見ながら、言語変化の理解には現代英語のヴァリエーションへの意識が不可欠であることを学ぶ。

11　　A few years ago, a new word appeared in English: *Ms*, variously pronounced 'miz' or 'muss'.

　本書の初版が出版されたのは 1994 年である。A few years ago となっているが、現在では Ms は定着した英語表現である。とはいえ、Ms の使用が 20 世紀後半以降に顕著に拡大してきたことには変わりない。*The Oxford English Dictionary* では、20 世紀の半ば以降の引用例がある。

練習問題 1（レベル 1）
Ms の他にも、ジェンダーへの意識が英語に与えた影響があるか、議論してみよう。ジェンダーへの意識は、日本語にも変化をもたらしたか、具体的な事例を挙げながら議論してみよう。

p.2

20　　English was introduced to North America from Britain in the seventeenth-century.

アメリカ英語とイギリス英語の違いについて、その全貌を概観した著書としては Tottie (2002), *An Introduction to American English* を紹介したい。また近年は、コーパスを利用して、アメリカ英語とイギリス英語の違いについて、個別のテーマを掘り下げる研究が多数刊行されている。

練習問題 2（レベル 1）
アメリカ英語とイギリス英語の発音・語彙・文法について、本文中で述べられているものの他にどのような違いがあるか、具体例を挙げてみよう。

練習問題 3（レベル 1）
オーストラリア英語、アイルランド英語など、英米以外の英語についても、その具体的な特徴を整理してみよう。

練習問題 4（レベル 3）
有名な文学作品等では、アメリカ英語版とイギリス英語版が存在することがある。このような作品を用いて、英語に違いがあるか分析してみよう。同様に、同じニュースを扱った英米の新聞を使用して、英米語の違いを調査してみよう。

練習問題 5（レベル 3）
英語の異なる変種を話す話者が言葉を交わしながら会話をする場面では、変種間の違いがどのような形で表出するだろうか。インターネットでインタビューなどの実例を探すか、被験者の許可をもらって実際の会話を観察・分析してみよう。

33　　two varieties of English

一般に variety とは同一言語内の異なる変種のことを言う。ここでの two varieties of English は、アメリカ英語とイギリス英語のこと。しかし、アメリカ英語やイギリス英語は、それぞれにまた多様な varieties を内包している。

> **練習問題 6（レベル 2）**
> Upton & Widdowson（2006）, *An Atlas of English Dialects* を用いて、現代イギリス英語の方言について意識を深めてみよう。方言地図を見た際の驚きや気づきを、グループで議論してみよう。

34　　As we shall see later, the combination of language change and geographical separation can have far-reaching consequences.

ここでは言語変化と地理的な隔たりの結果として、アメリカ英語とイギリス英語が異なる性質を帯びるようになってきたことに焦点が当てられている。しかし現在では、国際社会におけるアメリカの影響力やメディアの力により、アメリカ英語がイギリス英語を含むその他の英語に影響を与える傾向も観察されている。Unit 9 の終わりにある "After many centuries of slow divergence among regional varieties of English, the tendency is now largely the other way: towards a levelling of English everywhere, and a reduction in regional diversity"（p.48）という記述も参照。

> **練習問題 7（レベル 3）**
> イギリス英語がアメリカ英語の影響を受けて変化しているとされる現象の一つに insist や request などに続く that 節内で使用される仮定法の増加がある。グループで、
>
> > Hundt（1998）, "It is Important that this Study（*Should*）*Be* Based on the Analysis of Parallel Corpora: On the Use of Mandative Subjunctive in Four Major Varieties of English"
> > Crawford（2009）, "The Mandative Subjunctive"
> > Peters（2009）, "The Mandative Subjunctive in Spoken English"
>
> を分担して読み、現代英語の仮定法でどのような変化が起こっているか、議論してみよう。論文の詳細は、注釈の参考文献（pp.127-130）を参照。

p.4

1　　The 1990 edition of the *Longman Register of New Words* lists over a thousand new English words recorded for the first time in 1988-90.

一般に文法の変化には気づきにくいが、語彙の変化（増加）は認識されやすい。また、新たな語彙が何らかのきっかけで急速に広がることもある。

> 練習問題 8（レベル 1）
> EXERCISE 1.1 に挙げられた語彙について、1988 年以前に出版された辞書を使って、確認してみよう。

35　　In fact, these are just two of thousands of English words borrowed from French, a few of the others being *castle, government, country, army, beef, roast, fool, fruit, letter, horrible, gentle* and *mirror*.

　英語では、外国語から語彙を取り入れるときに borrow という動詞を使う。また、取り入れられた語のことを、loanword（借用語）と言う。英語は世界のさまざまな言語から多数の語彙を借りた、借用語が多い言語である。フランス語からの借用は、特にノルマン征服が起こった 1066 年以降に顕著である。借用語全般については Unit 3 (pp.12–18)、英語とフランス語の接触については Unit 14 の終わり (p.79) でも触れられている。

　なお、近年は英語の語彙が日本語を含む世界の言語に波及する傾向も顕著で、Algeo (1980), "Where Do All the New Words Come from?" は、英語が逆に語彙を「貸す」側に回っているという興味深い指摘を行っている (p.271)。

> 練習問題 9（レベル 1）
> ここに挙げられたフランス語からの借用語を *The Oxford English Dictionary* で調べ、語源情報や初出年代を確認してみよう。

> 練習問題 10（レベル 2）
> フランス語から英語に入った語彙には、他にどのようなものがあるか、本文中のもの以外にも 100 語ほど追加して、リストを作成してみよう。さらに、その語彙がどのような分野に集中しているか、グループで議論してみよう。

> 練習問題 11（レベル 1）
> 英語を含むヨーロッパの言語から日本語にどのような語が借用語として定着しているか、具体例を挙げながら、グループで議論してみよう。

p.7　Unit 2. ENGLISH IN THE PAST

1　　As we look at older and older samples of English, the language becomes increasingly difficult and strange, and the earliest English is an utterly foreign language to us. In a thousand years, English has changed beyond recognition.

　どのような言語も生きた言語である限り変化する、というのが本書の中心的なテーマである。中でも英語は、比較的短時間に大きく変化した言語の一つである。このユニットでは、少しずつ時代をさかのぼる形で、Modern English（近代英語、1500 年

頃～)、Middle English(中英語、1100年頃～1500年頃)、Old English(古英語、～1100年頃)という時代区分が紹介される。The earliest English is an utterly foreign language to us と書かれているように、古英語となると、英語の母語話者でも外国語のように感じるほど現代英語とは異なっている。

[**練習問題 12(レベル 1)**
YouTube で古英語の発音を聞くことができるサイトを探し、実際に聞いてみよう。

11　　As I remember, Adam, it was upon this fashion bequeathed me by will but poor a thousand crowns … that differs not from the stalling of an ox?

引用されているのは、*As You Like It*(『お気に召すまま』)の冒頭の部分。若干の分かりにくさはあるものの、EXERCISE 2.0(p.8)のヒントを利用すれば、解釈はほぼ可能であろう。3行目では、二人称単数の代名詞 thou がまだ使用されており、動詞はこれに呼応して、sayest となっている。

p.8
24　　Here we have an example of a change in English grammar which has occurred between Shakespeare's time and our own: modern English absolutely requires *Do you call that a good record?*, or, more informally, *Call that a good record?*

専門用語としての Modern English(通常は Modern の M も大文字)は1500年頃からとされるので、William Shakespeare(1564-1616)の英語は Modern English である。ここでの modern English は m が小文字で書かれていることからも分かるように、現在の英語の意味で使われている。疑問文や否定文で使用される助動詞の do が英語に浸透し始めるのは中英語の終わり頃からであり、1700年頃まで数百年をかけながら、do は徐々に英語に定着する。助動詞の do が導入される以前は、本文中に記述されているように、動詞と主語の倒置によって疑問文を作った。また否定文についても、p.7 の引用の最後の文、that differs not from the stalling of an ox も、現代英語なら that does not differ …のように do を使用するところであろう。

[**練習問題 13(レベル 2)**
本動詞の have が疑問文や否定文になるときに助動詞 do が使用されるかどうかについては、地域差があると言われている。特に、イギリス英語とアメリカ英語での使い方の違いが強調されることが多い。文法書等を参照しながら、整理してみよう。

[**練習問題 14(レベル 1)**
W. Shakespeare の First Folio は、ファクシミリ版(図書館利用)やインターネット上に公開されている複数のサイト等で読むことができる[*]。First Folio の *As You Like It*

と本文(p.7)の抜粋を比較してみよう。どのような違いがあるか、グループで議論してみよう。

    *たとえば、The Bodleian First Folio(https://firstfolio.bodleian.ox.ac.uk/)では、Downloads のところから作品ごとに画像を表示させることが可能である。

練習問題 15(レベル 3)

疑問文や否定文における助動詞 do の定着は、動詞によってその速度が違うと言われている。たとえば、know や doubt など、いくつかの動詞は、比較的遅くまで do を使用しない構文を好んだとされる。Brigham Young University の Mark Davies が公開するコーパスの中から、Early English Books Online Corpus(https://corpus.byu.edu/eebo/)を利用して、1650 年頃のいくつかの動詞の do の使用状況を調べてみよう。

練習問題 16(レベル 3)

W. Shakespeare の作品の一つを選び、動詞ごとに助動詞 do の使用状況を調べてみよう。(W. Shakespeare の作品については、練習問題 14 の注を参照。)

28   Shakespeare wrote about four hundred years ago, but the English he used is still called by scholars EARLY MODERN ENGLISH.

Early Modern English(初期近代英語)とは、1500 年頃～1700 年頃の英語のことを言う。ただし初期近代英語の年代設定は、研究者によって若干の違いがある。初期近代英語期は、上で取り上げた助動詞 do の定着のように、かなり大きな言語変化が起こった時代である。W. Shakespeare の他にも、この時期の代表として、イングランド王 James I(スコットランド王 James VI)が編纂させた Authorized Version of the English Bible(または King James Bible、1611)(欽定英訳聖書)がある。寺澤(2013),『聖書でたどる英語の歴史』には、W. Shakespeare の英語と欽定英訳聖書の英語の違いについて、興味深い比較がある(p.27)。

練習問題 17(レベル 2)

寺澤(2013),『聖書でたどる英語の歴史』の第 2 章を読みながら、欽定英訳聖書の英語と現代英語の比較を行い、両者の違いを議論してみよう。

30   Geoffrey Chaucer

Geoffrey Chaucer は、14 世紀の英国の作家・詩人。生年は 1340 年頃、没年は 1400 年である。ここで引用されている *The Canterbury Tales*(『カンタベリ物語』)は、未完ではあるが G. Chaucer が書き残した作品の中で最も有名である。他にも、*Troilus and Criseyde*(『トロイルスとクリセイデ』)などがある。

32 　　They were written in about 1387; …

　The Canterbury Tales の制作年代は 14 世紀であるが、現存するテキストは 15 世紀以降に書き写された写本である。したがって、ここに掲載されている中英語テキストは、G. Chaucer が使用した英語よりも若干新しい可能性がある。転写の作業を行った写字生(scribe)たちは、その過程で自分の英語に引き寄せてテキストを変更することが多かった。

35 　　But first I pray yow, of youre curteisye …

　現代英語訳である Wright(2011), *The Canterbury Tales* から該当の個所を引用すると、以下のようになる。

　　But first I beg you, not to put it down
　　To my ill-breeding if my speech be plain
　　When telling what they looked like, what they said,
　　Or if I use the exact words they used.
　　For, as you all must know as well as I,
　　To tell a tale told by another man
　　You must repeat as nearly as you can
　　Each word, if that's the task you've undertaken,
　　However coarse or broad his language is;
　　Or, in the telling, you'll have to distort it
　　Or make things up, or find new words for it. (p.21)

練習問題 18 (レベル 2)
G. Chaucer の英語を上の現代英語訳と比較対照し、その違いをグループで議論してみよう。

p.9

8 　　MIDDLE ENGLISH

　Middle English (中英語) の年代設定についても、先ほどの初期近代英語期と同様で、研究者によって若干異なることがある。一般には、ノルマン征服 (1066 年) と William Caxton による印刷技術の導入 (1476 年) を意識して、1100 年頃〜 1500 年頃とされることが多い。

練習問題 19 (レベル 1)
各種参考書を利用して、W. Caxton という人物について調べてみよう。

19 　　the word *arette*, for example, meant 'consider', 'reckon', and its strangely formed

negative *narette*, which occurs in this passage, therefore meant 'not to consider'.

narette は、ne arette が縮約を起こしたもので、ne は否定文を作るために動詞の前に置く否定の副詞(現代英語の not に相当)。ちなみにこの文は、ye narette it nat my vileynye というように否定の副詞の nat(現代英語 not)も含み、二重否定の構文になっている。古英語・中英語では、複数の否定語を同一の文に含む場合も、原則として意味は肯定にならずに否定のままであった。参考までに、否定語が 3 つ以上含まれる場合もあるので、より一般的な multiple negation または negative concord(多重否定)という用語を用いることもある。

練習問題 20(レベル 3)
現代英語でも、African American Vernacular English(AAVE)など、変種によっては多重否定が起こることがある。まず、AAVE とはどのような言語か調べてみよう。次に、Howe(2005), "Negation in African American Vernacular English" を読み、多重否定にはどのようなパターンが見られるか、整理してみよう。

23   Another major problem, but one which is difficult to demonstrate here, is Chaucer's pronunciation. In 1400 the pronunciation of English was astonishingly different from the pronunciation of today.

この時期の発音が現代英語のものと大きく異なっている要因の一つに、Great Vowel Shift(大母音推移)と呼ばれる現象がある。中英語の終わり頃から近代英語期にかけて長い時間をかけながら進行した長母音の推移で、現在でも地域によっては、この変化がまだ継続中だとされる。

練習問題 21(レベル 1)
大母音推移とはどのような変化か、調べてみよう。(一般的な英語史の教科書等、参考文献多数。)

34   OLD ENGLISH

Old English(古英語)は一般に 1100 年頃までの英語のことを言う。しかし、その始まりは 450 年頃とするものと 700 年頃とするものがある。前者は、アングル人、サクソン人、ジュート人がブリテン島に渡ったと伝えられる 449 年を英語の始まりとするもので、後者は英語で書かれた文献が現れるようになる頃からを古英語期とする考え方である。アングル人、サクソン人、ジュート人のブリテン島への渡来については、本文 Unit 9(p.46)の冒頭の記述およびその注(p.113)も参照。

35   *Anglo-Saxon Chronicle*

日本語では、『アングロ・サクソン年代記』。古英語期に King Alfred(アルフレッド

大王)のもとで編纂が始まり、中英語期に入ってからも編纂が続けられた。1154年の記述が最終である。内容の重複を含む複数の写本が現存する。大沢(2012)、『アングロ・サクソン年代記』を参照。

> **練習問題 22(レベル 2)**
> 本文中の *Anglo-Saxon Chronicle* とその現代英語訳を使用して、言語的な連続性と両者の差異について、グループで議論をしてみよう。

p.10

> **練習問題 23(レベル 1)**
> SUMMARY のところにある3つの文について、Unit 2 の記述を参考にしながら、内容を追加し、それぞれ10行程度の文章にまとめてみよう。

p.11

14　　Paston letters

　英国ノーフォークのパストン家で、中英語後期から数世代にわたって取り交わされた書簡。大英図書館所蔵。Norman Davis の編集による中英語の書簡(Davis(1958, 1971)または Davis(2004), *Paston Letters and Papers of the Fifteenth Century*)が使いやすい。著者名が明確であるなど文献としての位置づけもはっきりとしているため、中英語研究の題材として取り上げられることが多い。たとえば Bergs(2005), *Social Networks and Historical Sociolinguistics: Studies in Morphosyntactic Variation in the Paston Letters*(*1421-1503*)は、歴史社会言語学的な観点から、パストン家の第一世代(William I, Agnes)、第二世代(John I, Margaret, Edmond I, Elizabeth, William II, Clement II)、第三世代(John II, John III, Margery, Edmond II, Walter, William III)の書簡の英語を分析する。社本(1999)、『中世イギリスに生きたパストン家の女性たち―同家書簡集から』も、パストン家の人々が生きた当時の社会状況が分かって興味深い。

p.12　Unit 3.　**BORROWING WORDS**

1　　　　Speakers of a language may 'borrow'(that is, copy)words from other languages which they have encountered. English has borrowed many thousands of words from other languages, and is still doing so today.

　外国語から語彙や文構造等を取り入れて自らの言語の一部とすることに対して、borrow という言い方をし、借用された語は、loanword と言う。すでに、Unit 1 に付した注でもこの点に触れた(p.98)。ここにも書かれているように、実際には返却を意図しているわけではないので、借用という用語は、本来ならば必ずしも適当ではないかもしれない。

> **練習問題 24（レベル 1）**
> 本文中に、raccoon が英語で使用されるようになった経緯についての解説がある。*The Oxford English Dictionary* で raccoon を調べ、その例文にどのような特徴があるか議論してみよう。

p.13

7　　The name of another familiar beverage has made a similar journey. … and the ancient Ethiopian name finally passed into English in the form *coffee*.

　このパラグラフでは、coffee が英語の語彙となった過程が記述されている。このように食文化を豊かにする過程で、英語の中に取り入れられた借用語も多い。

> **練習問題 25（レベル 1）**
> *The Oxford English Dictionary* の coffee のところに書かれている情報（語源および例文を含む）を見て、coffee という語彙の歴史を、自分の方法で記述してみよう。

> **練習問題 26（レベル 2）**
> 他にも、食文化にかかわる英語の語彙の歴史について、それぞれにテーマを設定して調べてみよう。

p.15

5　　for a long time, French was a more prestigious language than English, and English speakers were often eager to show off their command of this prestigious language.

　フランス語からの借用が顕著になるのは、中英語後期である。中英語期のイングランド社会は、英語、フランス語、ラテン語が併用される多言語社会で、それぞれの言語に、異なる社会的意味合いがあった。ほぼ同義の単語が複数存在する場合（たとえば、本来語の time、フランス語系の age、ラテン語系の epoch）には、どの語を選択するかで若干の意味の違いや文体上の違いが出てくることがある。一般に、フランス語系の語彙には高級感があり、ラテン語系の語彙には学問的な響きがあると言われている。

12　　Even the familiar word *face* was borrowed from French into English

　一般に、基本語彙は本来語であることが多い。ここでは、そのような身近な語彙の中にも、借用語があることが強調されている。

15　　Today, however, the shoe is on the other foot.

　The shoe is on the other foot とは、「立場が逆転している」ことを言う。このパラグラフで述べられているように、現在では、日本語も含めて世界の言語が、多数の語彙

を英語から借用している。この点については、Unit 1 の注も参照（p.98）。

30　　　… in France, where the authorities are constantly making efforts to stamp out the use of English borrowings.

ここに書かれているように、できるだけ借用語を使用しないようにするための努力にもかかわらず、現在では、英語起源の語彙はフランス語にも流入している。

練習問題 27（レベル 1）
本文では、英語の語彙がさまざまな言語に借用されていることが述べられている。どのような分野に英語の語彙が浸透しているか、日本語の場合で考えてみよう。

練習問題 28（レベル 1）
フランス語が、その言語の特性を維持するために行ってきた言語政策の歴史を調べてみよう。英語についても同様の言語政策があったか、具体的に調べてみよう。

練習問題 29（レベル 3）
本文の EXERCISE 3.1 では、日本語と英語とでは発音の体系が異なるために英語からの借用語の発音が日本語の体系に合わせて調整されてきたことについて述べられている。日本語は、異なる時代に異なる語彙を世界の言語から借用してきたが、時代によって語彙の発音がどのように変化したか、調べてみよう。

練習問題 30（レベル 3）
日本語から英語に借用された語彙についても調べてみよう。どのような時代に、どのような語彙が英語に入ったかを調べて、その傾向について議論してみよう。

p.19　Unit 4．CREATING WORDS

1　　　English, like other languages, has a wide variety of devices for creating new words from its existing resources, including compounding, prefixation and suffixation, as well as more unusual devices.

このユニットでは、一般に word formation（語形成）と呼ばれる現象を扱う。言語には、派生や複合など、さまざまな方法で、新たな語彙を創出する力が備わっている。英語は、Unit 3 で扱った借用の他にも、語形成によって語彙を増大させてきた。特に古英語は、語形成能力に優れていたと言われる。時代が下るにしたがって、語形成より借用の比率が高まったとされるが、現代英語でも語形成能力は失われてはいない。

11   COMPOUNDING

　compound がここでは動詞で使用されているが、このプロセスによって完成した語を示す名詞も、英語では compound(複合語)である。複合語の中には、経年により摩耗が進み、複合語であると意識しにくいものもある。たとえば、gospel(古英語の god spel からで、その意味は 'good tidings')、lord(古英語の hlafweard からで、その意味は 'bread keeper')や daisy(古英語の dæges eage からで、その意味は 'day's eye')などは、その典型的な例である。

p.20

23   DERIVATION

　複合が、自立した二つ以上の語を組み合わせるのに対して、derivation(派生)では、核となる語に prefix(接頭辞)や suffix(接尾辞)を付加することで意味を拡張させ、新たな語を作る。prefix と suffix を合わせて affix(接辞)と言う。affix は、いわば語を作り出すためのパーツであって、それ自体は自立的に使用することができないので、bound morpheme(bound form)(拘束形態素)と呼ばれる。これは、自立的に使用することのできる free morpheme(free form)(自由形態素)に対する用語である。これらの専門用語については、寺澤(2002)、『英語学要語辞典』、赤野・他(2015)、『最新英語学・言語学用語辞典』も参照。

> **練習問題 31(レベル 1)**
> 本文中に示された接尾辞の -ness, -ful, -ous, -less, -ic が付加された派生語にはどのようなものがあるか、リストを作成してみよう。

> **練習問題 32(レベル 1)**
> 派生のために使用する接頭辞や接尾辞には、古英語以来のものと、フランス語やラテン語から借用したものがある。整理してみよう。

p.21

29   BACK-FORMATION

　A New English Dictionary(現在の *The Oxford English Dictionary*)の編集主幹を務めた James Murray(1837-1915)の用語と言われており、通常は「逆成」という訳語が与えられる。ここに挙げられた例以外で有名なものに、difficulty から生じた difficult がある。寺澤(2002)、『英語学要語辞典』、赤野・他(2015)、『最新英語学・言語学用語辞典』も参照。

p.25   Unit 5. CHANGE IN PRONUNCIATION

1　　　Like other aspects of language, pronunciation changes over time. Such change is largely responsible for the existence of different 'accents'—that is, different ways of pronouncing a language.

一般に、accent は発音上のヴァリエーションについての用語である。それ以外の言語上のヴァリエーションについては、dialect を使用する。

11 Hence, *every* speaker of English has an accent.

accent の訳語として「訛り」を挙げている辞書も少なくないが、本来、accent はすべての話者がもっているものであるので、誤解を避けるために、「アクセント」と呼ぶことにする。ただし日常的には、accent がいわゆる「標準的な」発音以外の発音の意味で使用されることもある。

p.26

3 If you pronounce these pairs identically, you have what linguists call a NON-RHOTIC accent. If you pronounce them differently, you probably have a RHOTIC accent.

一般に r の音を響かせるのはアメリカ英語の特徴で、イギリス英語では r を発音しないとされるが、rhotic, non-rhotic の違いは、ここに書かれているように複雑である。イギリスでも r の脱落が進んでいない地域(すなわち rhotic の地域)は多い。この現象は母音のあとの r に起こるので、post-vocalic r とも呼ばれる。

> **練習問題 33（レベル 2）**
>
> post-vocalic r は、Romaine (2000), *Language in Society: An Introduction to Sociolinguistics* の "Change in real v. apparent time" (pp.150-155) の部分でも取り上げられている。この箇所を読んで、その要点をまとめてみよう。なお、apparent time については、Unit 13 の注(p.124)も参照。

> **練習問題 34（レベル 2）**
>
> 本文中に "An innovation appears in one spot and may be taken up by other speakers" (l. 34) という記述がある。日本語または英語から、これを説明するのに適した事例を取り上げて議論してみよう。

p.31 Unit 6. CHANGE IN SPELLING

1 English spelling is complex and irregular, and it has only been largely fixed since the eighteenth century. Much of this complexity derives from our custom of spelling words as they were pronounced centuries ago, rather than as they are pronounced now.

英語の綴り字が不規則であることには、このユニットで述べられているように、歴

史が関係している場合が多い。音韻変化が起こる前の発音を反映した綴り字になっている場合、特定の地域の発音を綴り字だけが残している場合、フランス人の写字生やオランダ人の植字工の綴り字の慣習がもち込まれた場合、ラテン語やギリシャ語の語源を反映するように綴り字を「正しく」改めた場合など、多様な要因が背景にある。

英語の綴り字の歴史全般についてさらに詳しく学びたい場合は、Horobin (2013), *Does Spelling Matter?*（日本語訳は、堀田 (2017),『スペリングの英語史』）を参照。

練習問題 35（レベル 2）
本文の冒頭に発音が同じで綴り字が異なる例として、flour と flower が挙げられている。*The Oxford English Dictionary* を利用して、この二つの単語の使い方や綴り字の歴史を調べるとともに、辞書内に引用されている例文も観察してみよう。

p.32

6　Most people today seem reluctant to consider any modifications in our admittedly perplexing spelling ...

現実的には、ここに述べられている通りであるが、歴史を見ると、英語の綴り字改革の運動は何度も起こった。そのほとんどが失敗に終わっている。綴り字改革の歴史全般については、山口 (2009),『英語の改良を夢みたイギリス人たち—綴り字改革運動史 1834-1975』を参照。

練習問題 36（レベル 2）
英語の綴り字改革の歴史について、詳しく調べてみよう。

33　þ = modern English *th*

ルーン文字から採用した文字で thorn と呼ばれ、現代英語の th に相当。古英語・中英語で広く用いられる。他にも th の発音を表す文字として、ð (eth)（大文字は Ð）が使用されることがある。これらの文字は、p.9 の古英語文献の引用のところで既出。また、ルーン文字とローマ文字については、Unit 9 の注 (p.114) も参照。

練習問題 37（レベル 2）
EXERCISE 6.0 で与えられた単語の中から、cwen, heofon, geong, brycg, sceal について、現代英語の綴り字を用いて *The Oxford English Dictionary* を引き、それぞれの綴り字の歴史を整理してみよう。

p.33

29　One major factor in the fixing of English spelling was the introduction of printing in the fifteenth century.

W. Caxton により印刷技術がイギリスに導入されたのは、1476 年のことである。これにより、綴り字が定着の方向に向かったのは事実であるが、W. Caxton 自身、さまざまな綴り字の中からどの綴り字を採用すべきか苦悩しており、本当の意味での綴り字の定着にはしばらく時間がかかった。なお、この時期に W. Caxton の印刷工房で働いていたオランダ人の植字工の影響で導入された綴り字もある。たとえば、ghost の gh がそれに当たる。

37   A significant but decidedly unhelpful intervention was made in some cases by scholars too eager to identify a connection with Latin.

このパラグラフでは、ルネサンス期に古典への関心が高まり、より語源に忠実な形に綴り字を改める動きが盛んになったことが述べられている。またこのような動きの中で、誤って黙字が導入されてしまうこともあった。island は、そのような綴り字の例としてよく知られている。なお語源的綴り字の導入は、一般にルネサンス期に特徴的な現象であると言われるが、その萌芽は、すでに中英語期にも観察できる。

練習問題 38（レベル 1）
中英語後期から初期近代英語期に導入された語源的綴り字には、本文中で言及されている debt, doubt, receipt の他にどのようなものがあるか、調べてみよう。

練習問題 39（レベル 2）
The Oxford English Dictionary を使って、island の綴り字の歴史を確認し、整理してみよう。

47   By the eighteenth century the standardization of English spelling was well advanced, but still not complete. It was in this century that the great English dictionaries appeared, the most important of which was Dr Samuel Johnson's magisterial work published in 1755. The influence of this dictionary was such that the spellings preferred by Dr Johnson came to be accepted in almost every case as the standard spelling in England.

S. Johnson (1709-1784) は、最初の本格的な英語辞書である *A Dictionary of the English Language* (1755) を刊行した他に、書簡なども残している。個人的な書き物では、必ずしも辞書と統一的な綴り字を使用しているとは言えないようで興味深い (cf. Osselton (1984), "Informal Spelling Systems in Early Modern English: 1500-1800")。この時期に至っても、まだ綴り字は完全に統一された段階には達していなかった。

練習問題 40（レベル 1）
アメリカ英語とイギリス英語の綴り字の違いについてまとめてみよう。また、その

練習問題 41（レベル 3）
Osselton(1984), "Informal Spelling Systems in Early Modern English: 1500-1800" を読んで、その内容を要約してみよう。

p.36　Unit 7. CHANGE IN GRAMMAR

1　The grammar of English has changed dramatically in the last thousand years. The most important changes took place centuries ago, but our grammar is continuing to change even today.

ここでの grammar は、語形変化や統語全般を包含する広い意味で使用されている。ただし、議論の中心はどちらかといえば統語論に置かれている。

p.37

4　(e) She gave it me. (f) She gave me it.
Upton & Widdowson(2006), *An Atlas of English Dialects*(pp.64-65) に give it me, give me it についての方言分布を示した分かりやすい情報がある。

練習問題 42（レベル 3）
Brigham Young University の Mark Davies(http://davies-linguistics.byu.edu/personal/) が提供する現代英語コーパスの一つを用いて、本文中にある She gave it me と She gave me it の生起状況を確認してみよう。

14　The familiar verb *go* formerly had an irregular past-tense form *yede* or *yode*. In about the fifteenth century, however, it acquired a new past-tense form: *went*.

このように語源の異なる語をもってきてパラダイムに据えることを suppletion（補充法）と言う。高頻度語によく見られる現象で、卑近なところでは、他にも be 動詞の変化形や、形容詞 good, bad の比較級、最上級を挙げることができる。

練習問題 43（レベル 1）
The Oxford English Dictionary を用いて、動詞 go の歴史を確認してみよう。

40　Most conspicuously, words in Old English changed their form for grammatical purposes far more than occurs in the modern language.

ここでは専門用語を避けた結果、記述がかえって分かりにくくなっている。簡単に述べると、古英語は、格変化が豊かな言語だったということである。現代ドイツ語と同様に、nominative（主格）、genitive（属格）（主に所有を表す格）、dative（与格）（主に間

接目的語を表す格)、accusative(対格)(主に直接目的語を表す格)があり、文法的な機能を格変化で表した。例として挙げられている se cyning は、形態が主格形であるので、動詞の後に置かれても主語であると判断できる。これに対して現代英語では、文法機能の多くを語順など、別の手段にゆだねざるを得なくなっている。

p.38

22　In more complex types of sentences, the passive could not be used; this was particularly so with the -*ing* form of the verb.

　ここで述べられていることは、厳密には受動構文の問題というよりも、進行形の問題である。進行形は、近代英語期に入ってから急速に拡大してきた構文で、現在もその使用の幅が広がっていると言われている。進行形が十分に定着していない時代には、進行形と受動態を組み合わせる、進行形と完了構文を組み合わせるなどの複雑な構文はまだ起こらない。このため、ここで述べられているような構文が英語に現れるようになるのは比較的遅い。

p.39

9　The most dramatic changes occurred before the end of the Middle Ages, but further changes in grammar are occurring even today.

　コーパスを使用した現代英語研究が広がり、現在では現代英語の「変化」に焦点を当てた研究も盛んである。

> **練習問題 44(レベル 3)**
> 20世紀の英語の変化を扱った論文の一つ、Leech & Smith(2009), "Change and Constancy in Linguistic Change: How Grammatical Usage in Written English Evolved in the Period 1931–1991" を読んで、現代英語の文法にどのような変化が起こっているか、要点をまとめてみよう。また可能であれば、そのうちのどれかの文法項目について、自由に文献資料を定めて調査を行い、さらに掘り下げてみよう。

p.40

> **練習問題 45(レベル 3)**
> EXERCISE 7.4 の(a), (d), (g)より、W. Shakespeare の時代の英語では、疑問文や否定文を作る際の助動詞 do の使用が確立していないことが分かる。W. Shakespeare (または、その同時代)の作品を用いて、助動詞 do の使用状況について調べてみよう。なお、W. Shakespeare の First Folio については、Unit 2 の注(pp.99–100)を参照。

> **練習問題 46（レベル 3）**
> EXERCISE 7.4 の(a), (h)より、W. Shakespeare の時代の英語では、三人称単数現在の動詞の語尾として -th と -s の両方があることが分かる。W. Shakespeare（または、その同時代）の作品を用いて -th と -s のヴァリエーションを調査し、このテーマをさらに掘り下げてみよう。

p.41　Unit 8.　CHANGE IN MEANING

1　　Like other aspects of language, the meanings of words can change over time. Two common types of change are broadening and narrowing of meaning, but many other types can occur.

　伝統的な英語史では、意味の broadening と narrowing（本文中では、それぞれについて generalization（一般化）と specialization（特殊化）という専門用語が紹介される）に加えて、amelioration（向上）と deterioration（堕落）に言及し、意味変化の代表的な 4 つのパターンとして紹介されることが多い。たとえば silly は、本来は「祝福された」という良い意味を有していたが、現在では「愚かな」という意味で使用されるので、意味の堕落の例であるとされる。その他にも、意味の subjectification（主観化）や abstraction（抽象化）などがある。

> **練習問題 47（レベル 1）**
> 英語またはその他の言語について、意味の generalization, specialization の例と思われるものを、さらに挙げてみよう。

4　　On a Sunday in 1948 …

　このパラグラフでは、20 世紀になって gay の意味に急速な変化が起こり、本来の「陽気な」意味では使用されなくなった過程が紹介されている。Burridge (2004), *Weeds in the Garden of Words: Further Observations on the Tangled History of the English Language* の "History of 'gay'"（pp.58-60）にも、この単語の多様な意味と近年の意味変化について分かりやすい記述がある。

> **練習問題 48（レベル 2）**
> *The Oxford English Dictionary* で gay の項目を調べ、その多様な意味と歴史を、引用例も参考にしながら確認してみよう。

p.42

31　　EUPHEMISMS

　婉曲表現のこと。本文中で "polite but roundabout expressions for things which are considered too nasty to talk about directly" と説明されている通り。

注釈　113

44　　　Sex is another area in which euphemisms flourish.

　このユニットでは、性にかかわる語として、gay と intercourse が挙げられている。どちらも、最初は性に限定された語ではなく、ごく一般的な語であった。しかし、一旦性的な意味を帯びると、それ以外の場面で使用することが避けられるようになり、ますます性的な意味に限定されていく傾向が見られる。

p.44

> **練習問題 49（レベル 1）**
> EXERCISE 8.3 で metaphor という用語が使用されている。metaphor と合わせて、metonymy, synecdoche, simile などの用語についても、言語学辞典等を使用して、確認しておこう。

p.45

> **練習問題 50（レベル 2）**
> EXERCISE 8.4 では、左側の単語の本来の意味を選ぶことになっているが、それぞれの単語について、その意味変化の歴史を簡単に説明してみよう。

p.46　Unit 9. THE ORIGIN OF DIALECTS

1　　　The combination of language change and geographical separation inevitably results in the rise of regional dialects; if no unifying force intervenes, dialects may diverge from one another without limit.

　Unit 9 から Unit 11 にかけては、英語の起源にかかわる記述となっている。Unit 9 では、英語のもとになる言語がヨーロッパ大陸からブリテン島にもたらされた以降のこと、Unit 10 では、これより少しだけさかのぼって、英語と近い親戚関係にあるゲルマン諸語のこと、そして Unit 11 では、さらにさかのぼって、インド・ヨーロッパ語族全般について議論されている。背景にある考え方は、同じ言語でも時間の経過とともに、その言語の中に方言差が生じ、これが次第に独立して、新たな言語を生み出すというものである。方言と言語の連続性については、Unit 10 および Unit 14 でも触れられている。

5　　　The ancestral form of English was brought to Britain from the fifth century onwards, by peoples migrating from the northwest of the continent of Europe, from areas that are now part of the Netherlands, Germany and Denmark. ... Anglish, or English.

　聖職者・歴史家であった Venerable Bede（673?-735）の著作、*Historia Ecclesiastica*

Gentis Anglorum（日本語訳は、高橋(2008)、『ベーダ英国民教会史』）に、ゲルマン人がイングランドに渡来したのは 449 年と記されている。ただし現在では、これよりも早い時期にゲルマン人がイングランドに入っていたことに触れる英語史も多い。たとえば、Brinton & Arnovick(2017), *The English Language: A Linguistic History*(pp.154-156) を参照。

練習問題 51（レベル 1）
The Oxford English Dictionary を使って、England という語の歴史を確認しよう。

15　By the early eighth century, however, English was beginning to be written in a form of the Roman alphabet

　古代ゲルマン社会で使用されていた文字は、ルーン文字と呼ばれるもので、特にイギリスで使用されていたものを Anglo-Saxon runes と言う。しかしながら、キリスト教とともにローマ文字がもたらされると、ローマ文字を使用することが一般的となる。ルーン文字については、河崎(2017)、『ルーン文字の起源』を参照。

23　That is, in the space of three or four centuries, significant dialect differences had arisen in English.

　この記述は、少し誤解を招く可能性がある。このユニットの最初に書かれているように、ブリテン島に英語のもとになる言語がもたらされたときから、複数のゲルマン民族が英語の形成にかかわっており、すでに方言差のようなものが存在していたと考えられている。ただし、これはブリテン島における方言の形成そのものを否定するものではない。本文 p.47 の古英語の方言についての注も参照(pp.114-115)。

25　In an age when travel was mostly on foot, or occasionally on horseback, and no message could be sent faster than a human being could carry it, communication between widely separated areas was slow and infrequent. As a result, linguistic changes appearing in one part of the country could spread only very slowly, and three or four centuries was ample time for the accumulated weight of such changes to bring about substantial regional differences in English.

　一般に、人々の行き来が少ないと、言語は他の地域で起こっている言語変化から取り残される傾向があると言われる。すなわち、言語変化と社会の在り方は密接にかかわっている。Milroy(2003), "On the Role of the Speaker in Language Change" を参照。

p.47
7　Northumbrian(spoken in northern England and southern Scotland), Mercian(in the Midlands), West Saxon(in the southwest) and Kentish(in the southeast).

伝統的に、古英語の方言は、この4つに区分されることが多い。上述のようにゲルマン人がブリテン島に移住してきた段階から、異なるゲルマン民族の言語が方言差となって表れた。したがって、この4つの方言は、異なる民族が移住した地域と対応関係をもっている。Northumbrian と Mercian がアングル人の言葉をもとにしたものであり、West Saxon 方言はサクソン人の言葉、Kentish はジュート人の言葉を反映したものがもとになっている。

> **練習問題 52（レベル 1）**
> 古英語の方言について、Northumbrian, Mercian, West Saxon, Kentish の大まかな地図上の境界を調べてみよう

10　　For illustration, here is an extract from a famous Old English poem, the celebrated *Hymn* of the poet Caedmon, in two dialects.

ここでの引用は、方言の違いを実感するためのものであるが、参考までに Liuzza (2014), *Old English Poetry: An Anthology* (pp.18-19) の現代英語訳を以下に示す。

> Now let us praise Heaven-kingdom's guardian,
> the Maker's might and his mind's thoughts,
> the work of the glory-father — of every wonder,
> eternal Lord, He established a beginning.

28　　Throughout the Middle Ages, regional differences continued to develop, and by the fifteenth century, it is clear, English speakers from different parts of the country often had great difficulty in understanding one another.

当時の英語が多様であったことは、異なる地域の文献を比較すれば明らかであるが、当時の人々の陳述の中にも、地域による言語の多様性への気づきを読み取ることができる。W. Caxton が *Eneydos*(1490) に付けた序文の中で、egg の複数形として egges と eyren の両方が存在することに言及する一節は特に有名である。Blake (1973), *Caxton's Own Prose*(pp.78-81) を参照。実際には、方言が異なると理解できないとまでは言えない場合も多かったと考えられるが、少なくとも部分的には、異なる方言間で誤解が生じる可能性はあったのであろう。

p.48

16　　This is a far cry from the days when an English speaker only rarely encountered the English spoken fifty miles away.

たしかに、言語の方言を考えるに際には、距離だけではなく、コミュニケーションの手段や交通手段のあり方を無視することはできない。現在では、アメリカ英語の影響がイギリスにも及んでいる事例がたくさん報告されている。これには、世界におけ

るアメリカの位置づけも関係している。Unit 1 の注および練習問題(p.97)も参照。

p.49

28　However, the regional differences in the United States are much less marked than those in Britain, and moreover they are almost entirely confined to the eastern and southeastern parts of the country.

　この記述はたしかにその通りで、面積の割にはアメリカ英語の方言差は、イギリス英語に比べて少ないと言われている。しかし、アメリカでも移住にかかわる状況との関係から、興味深い方言的特徴が見られる地域もある。

> **練習問題 53（レベル 3）**
> アパラチアの英語は、アメリカ英語の地方色との関係で取り上げられることが多い。Montgomery(1997), "Making Transatlantic Connections between Varieties of English" を読んで、その内容を要約してみよう。また、動詞が直説法現在複数であるのに語尾に -s がつく現象（英語の方言に見られる現象）全般について調べてみよう。

p.51　Unit 10. RELATEDNESS BETWEEN LANGUAGES

1　Given sufficient time, the ordinary processes of language can split a single language not merely into dialects but into distinct languages. Languages which share a common origin of this kind are said to be genetically related. English is genetically related to a group of languages collectively known as the Germanic languages.

　すでに述べたように、時代の経過によって方言差が大きくなると、新たな言語の誕生につながることがある。Unit 10 では、系統図を少しさかのぼって、英語の祖先であるゲルマン諸語について観察を行う。

8　Given sufficient time, these DIALECTS (regional varieties) can diverge so much that they eventually become mutually incomprehensible and must at some point be regarded as different LANGUAGES.

　方言差が次第に大きくなってくると、新たな言語とみなした方がよい状況が生まれる。インド・ヨーロッパ語族の考え方は、想定されるインド・ヨーロッパ祖語が、このような過程を経て、次々に枝分かれを起こして新たな言語を生み出してきたというものである。そのうちの一つがゲルマン語、そしてこれを祖語として、さらに枝分かれした結果として、英語があると考えられている。英語史の記述では、インド・ヨーロッパ祖語から議論を始め、時代を徐々に下りながら、最終的に英語に到達するものが多い。一方、本書のアプローチは逆である。Unit 9 および Unit 11 の注（pp.113, 117）も参照。

p.52

7　　Ingvaeonic

北海沿岸のゲルマン語。タキトゥスに、この用語での言及がある。

24　　Others include Icelandic, Norwegian, Danish, Swedish, Faroese (in the Faroe Islands), German, Yiddish, Afrikaans (in South Africa) and Gothic (an extinct language formerly spoken by many of the barbarian peoples who invaded the Roman Empire).

ここまで来て、ようやくゲルマン語族の全貌が見えてきた。ゲルマン語族は一般に、東ゲルマン語のグループ、北ゲルマン語のグループ、西ゲルマン語のグループに分類される。ここに挙げられている言語では、Gothic が東ゲルマン語、Icelandic, Norwegian, Danish, Swedish, Faroese が北ゲルマン語、German, Yiddish, Afrikaans が西ゲルマン語である。英語も西ゲルマン語のグループに属する。

> 練習問題 54（レベル 1）
> Gothic, Yddish, Afrikaans は、それぞれどのような言語か調べてみよう。

p.54

> 練習問題 55（レベル 2）
> ここではゲルマン諸語の類似点を見るために、Old English, Old Saxon, Old High German, Old Icelandic, Gothic と Early Modern English の「主の祈り」が与えられている。しかし、Old English の「主の祈り」と Early Modern English の「主の祈り」の比較、すなわち通時的な比較も面白い。両者を比較して、気づくところを議論してみよう。

p.58　Unit 11. MORE REMOTE RELATIONS

1　　The Germanic family of languages to which English belongs is itself only one branch of a much larger family called the Indo-European family. All the languages in this family are descended from a single remote ancestor called Proto-Indo-European, spoken perhaps 6,000 years ago in eastern Europe.

ここで Proto-Indo-European（インド・ヨーロッパ祖語）と呼ばれている言語は、現在インドからヨーロッパにかけて広く分布する言語の祖先にあたると「想定」されている言語で、実際に文献資料が残っているわけではない。

> 練習問題 56（レベル 1）
> インド・ヨーロッパ語族にはどのような言語が含まれているか、できるだけ多数の

言語を取り上げて整理してみよう。

16　English and Spanish (Spanish is definitely not a Germanic language)
　ここでは英語とスペイン語の対比が課題となっている。スペイン語は、ラテン語、イタリア語、フランス語、ポルトガル語などとともにイタリック語派に属し、英語とはやや遠い親戚関係にある。

p.59
29　Some of the more important Romance languages are Spanish, Catalan and Galician (all spoken in Spain), Portuguese (in Portugal), French and Occitan (in France), Romansh (in part of Switzerland), Italian, Sardinian and Friulian (in Italy) and Rumanian (in Rumania).
　本文中に述べられているように、いずれもラテン語の子孫にあたる言語である。Unit 12 の EXERCISE 12.0 も参照。

> **練習問題 57（レベル 1）**
> ここに挙げられているロマンス諸語について、どのような言語か調べてみよう。

p.60
7　Almost all the modern languages of Europe, and also many of the languages of Asia, can trace their origin back to this same ancestral language.
　ヨーロッパのほとんどの言語はインド・ヨーロッパ祖語にさかのぼると言われているが、フィンランド語のように、インド・ヨーロッパ語族に属していない言語もヨーロッパには存在する。バスク語の起源もよく分からない。バスク語については、Unit 12 のバスク語についての注（p.123）も参照。

25　Since this great group of languages extends from India to western Europe, we call it the INDO-EUROPEAN family. And the remote ancestor of the Indo-European languages is, of course, called PROTO-INDO-EUROPEAN, or PIE for short.
　ここに述べられているように、インド・ヨーロッパ語族の言語はアジアにも広がっており、一大言語圏を形成している。

> **練習問題 58（レベル 2）**
> インド・ヨーロッパ語族の研究のきっかけとなった William Jones の講演、"The Third Anniversary Discourse" は、インターネット上で読むことができる。全文を読んでみよう*。また、W. Jones はどのような経歴の人であったか、調べてみよう。
> 　　* "The Third Anniversary Discourse" を読むことができるサイトとして、Internet Archive

（https://archive.org/stream/asiaticresearche01asia#page/414/mode/2up）を紹介しておきたい。

p.64　Unit 12.　THE BIRTH AND DEATH OF LANGUAGES

1　When two or more languages come into contact, it is possible for a new language to be born, or for some of the old languages to die out.

　これまでに見てきた系統発生のメカニズムとは別に、言語接触によって言語が生まれることもある。あるいは言語が死に絶えることもある。このユニットでは、言語接触によって生まれる contact languages（接触言語）に焦点が当てられている。

13　Of course, PIE itself must have been descended from a still more remote ancestor spoken at an even earlier period, but the data and the methods at our disposal are not sufficient to trace the history of the Indo-European family back any further.

　Unit 11 での記述はインド・ヨーロッパ祖語までさかのぼるところで終わりになっているが、実際は、この PIE でさえ、系統発生的な枝分かれによって生まれてきた言語の一つにすぎないことが、ここでは述べられている。

p.65

6　It happens when speakers of different languages come into contact and need to have extensive dealings with one another. Consider, for example, the case of New Guinea.

　ニューギニアの事例は、言語接触の典型的な事例としてしばしば取り上げられる。

> **練習問題 59（レベル 1）**
> ニューギニアの地理的環境、社会的環境、そして歴史について調べてみよう。

25　The resulting system in each area was what we call a PIDGIN: a reduced language stitched together from bits and pieces of other languages, showing a good deal of variation, with a limited capacity for expression.

　ピジンの定義は容易ではない。一般に、文法を提供する substratum（基層言語）と呼ばれる（現地の）言語の上に、superstratum（上層言語）と呼ばれる語彙提供言語（多くの場合はヨーロッパの言語）が覆いかぶさるようにして、接触言語が成立する場合が多い。

38　A creole is simply a former pidgin which has become somebody's mother tongue and which has been enriched and elaborated to the point where it is just like any other language.

　クレオールは、先のピジンが母語話者を獲得したもの。きわめて現地語の

substratum に近いものからきわめて上層語の superstratum に近いものまでが緩やかな層をなしていることが多く、その状態のことを creole continuum という用語で説明することもある。

> 練習問題 60（レベル 2）
> Schneider(1990), "The Cline of Creoleness in English-oriented Creoles and Semi-creoles of the Caribbean" は、クレオールの定義に始まり、クレオールにもさまざまな段階があることを、具体例とともに示した論文である。読んで、その内容を要約してみよう。

43　　This creole is called Tok Pisin(apparently from the English 'talk business'), and it is now the national language of Papua New Guinea.

　Tok Pisin は、接触言語の中で最も代表的なものの一つ。パプア・ニューギニアで使用され、すでにクレオール化している。語彙提供言語は英語。

> 練習問題 61（レベル 2）
> Tok Pisin の具体的な特徴を調べてみよう。

p.66

4　　One of the most striking examples is Haitian Creole, derived originally from French and several African languages; this is now the mother tongue of the entire population of Haiti.

　ハイチ語とも呼ばれる Haitian Creole は、本文に記述されている通り、フランス語との接触によって生じたクレオール。YouTube 上には、ハイチ語の話者の発音を実際に聞くことができるサイトが多数ある。

28　　Language death is a major feature of human history.

　言語が生まれる場合と同様、言語が消滅することについても生物のメタファーを用いて、language death（言語の死）と言う。多くの場合は、言語使用者が徐々に減少し、最後の母語話者がこの世を去ることで言語の死が起こる。また、母語話者の数が減少してきた言語を endangered languages（危機言語）と言う。

> 練習問題 62（レベル 1）
> 危機言語とされる言語にはどのようなものがあるか調べてみよう。

41　　Latin, in fact, has never 'died' — that is, there was never any time when people stopped speaking it.

ここに書かれているように、「言語の死」の定義は簡単そうに見えて、必ずしもそうではない。死語の代表的な例とされるラテン語は、このパラグラフの後半に書かれているように、フランス語、イタリア語、スペイン語などに分岐した形で現在も母語話者を有する。Swann, Deumert, Lillis & Mesthrie (2004), *A Dictionary of Sociolinguistics* も参照。

> **練習問題 63（レベル 2）**
> Nelson (2007), "Language Death" では、「言語の死」にいくつかのパターンがあることが、分かりやすく説明されている。読んで、その論点をまとめてみよう。

p.67

14　The case of Old English is similar, but not identical.

　ここに述べられているように、古英語も、現代英語とはまったく性質が異なり、現在では古英語をそのまま使用する母語話者はいない。その意味では、dead language である。しかしながら、多様な言語への分岐がなかったので、ラテン語の場合とは異なる見方をするのが一般的である。

22　In this unit, we are considering true language death: cases in which a language literally ceases to be spoken, and gives rise to no later forms at all.

　ここでは、上記のラテン語や古英語の場合とは違い、特定の言語を母語とする話者が死ぬ、あるいは他の言語に乗り換えることで話者がいなくなるなどの過程を経て、言語が死滅する場合を議論する。

> **練習問題 64（レベル 1）**
> 本文中にある Yahi Indians について調べてみよう。

p.68

26　Mrs Dolly Pentreath, who died in 1777, was possibly the last native speaker of Cornish, though some scholars believe a few others may have survived for another thirty years or so.

　この事例は、母語話者の数が減り、最後の母語話者が死ぬことで言語の死が起こる事例としてしばしば取り上げられる。

34　Manx lasted rather longer in the face of English pressure. It is reported that Mr Ned Maddrell, who died in 1974 at the age of 97, was the last native speaker of Manx.

　Manx は、マン島語。イングランドとアイルランドの間に位置するマン島の言語で、

ゲール語の一つ。

45　　The position of Irish is not much better. Two centuries ago, Irish was spoken by a majority of the Irish population; today, in spite of vigorous efforts by the Irish government to preserve the language, Irish as a mother tongue is close to extinction.

　現在のアイルランドでは、人口のほとんどが英語の母語話者であり、アイルランド語を母語とする人々の数は激減している。インターネット上に公開された Central Statistics Office (Cork, Ireland) の情報によれば、2016 年 4 月時点でのアイルランド語話者は 1,761,420 人で、人口の 39.8%。アイルランド語を話すことができる人々の割合は性別によって若干異なるようで、女性は 55%、男性は 45% となっている*。

　　* https://www.cso.ie/en/releasesandpublications/ep/p-cp10esil/p10esil/ilg/ を参照。

練習問題 65（レベル 1）
アイルランドで英語が使用されるようになった歴史的経緯について、調べてみよう。

p.69

3　　Scots Gaelic, once the first language throughout the Highlands, is now confined to the Western Isles and a few neighbouring parts of the mainland. There it is still the everyday language of perhaps 80,000 people, but virtually all of these are bilingual in English, and it is difficult to see a bright future for Gaelic.

　インターネット上には、2011 年のスコットランドの国勢調査の結果が公開されている*。これによると、スコットランドに住む 3 歳以上の人々でゲール語についての何らかの知識を有する人々は 87,100 人（人口の 1.7%）。一見すると、本文に記載の 80,000 人とそれほど変わらないようであるが、本文の記載は、everyday language とする人々についてのものである。国勢調査に戻ると、ゲール語を話すことができる人々は、57,600 人となっている。

　　* https://www.scotlandscensus.gov.uk/news/gaelic-analytical-report-part-1 を参照。

9　　Once the language of the entire population of Wales (and, before the Anglo-Saxon invasion, of England), Welsh is now spoken by only 18 per cent of Welsh people, totalling about 600,000 speakers, and all of them are bilingual in English.

　ウェールズ語については、インターネット上に公開されている National Survey for Wales, 2013-14: Welsh Language Use Survey によって、さらに詳しい情報を得ることができる*。これによると、2011 年の国勢調査では、ウェールズ語を話すのは、ウェールズに住む 3 歳以上の人々の 19% となっている。ただし、その後の調査で、これよりも高い比率が公開されているものがあるとの記載もある。

* http://www.comisiynyddygymraeg.cymru/English/Publications%20List/20150129%20DG%20S%20Welsh%20Language%20Use%20Survey%202013-14%20-%20Main%20report.pdf を参照。

38　The only exception to this obliteration of earlier languages is Basque. Spoken today by some 600,000 people at the western end of the Pyrenees, Basque has no living relatives, and it is the sole survivor of the ancient pre-Indo-European languages of western Europe.

バスク語については、Campbell & King (2013), *Compendium of the World's Languages* の概説 (pp.198-204) が簡潔で分かりやすい。また、本書の著者である R. L. Trask は、バスク語についての詳細な研究成果を著書として公刊している。さらに詳しい情報については、Trask (1997), *The History of Basque* を参照。

p.70

練習問題 66（レベル 1）
本文中にある Wappo や Mbabaram について、さらに詳しく調べてみよう。

練習問題 67（レベル 2）
本文では言語の死について、ヨーロッパの言語を中心に議論が進められてきたが、これに合わせて日本語の方言（母語話者が極端に少なくなった方言や皆無となった方言など）の問題を議論してみよう。

p.72　Unit 13. ATTITUDES TOWARDS LANGUAGE CHANGE

1　Throughout history, older and more conservative speakers have objected to changes in the language whenever they have noticed them. These attitudes are still with us today, but they rarely have much effect on the development of the language.

言語は、人々の文化や社会と密接に関係しており、人々は言語に対してさまざまな思いを抱く。言語変化が、人々にとっては堕落であると感じられる場合が多いことをこの文章は語っているが、ここに書かれているように、言語の変化を止めることは事実上不可能である。

練習問題 68（レベル 2）
日本語を例に、人々が言語変化についてどのような意識をもっているか、具体的な事例を挙げながら議論してみよう。

6 　　Hopefully we'll arrive in time for lunch. 　…　But around 1970 this new use of *hopefully* began to occur in British English, after establishing itself a few years earlier in the United States.

　文全体を修飾する hopefully のこの用法については、好意的な評価を与えない文法家もいる。しかしながら、Gatto (2014), *The Web as Corpus: Theory and Practice*, Chapter 3 の Google Books を用いたデータ (pp.94-95) によれば、hopefully のこの用法は 1960 年以降、急激な増加傾向を示している。

練習問題 69（レベル 3）
文全体を修飾する hopefully の用法が 20 世紀の後半になると文法に対して規範主義的な人々の目に留まるようになったことに言及する興味深い議論もある。Curzan (2014), *Fixing English: Prescriptivism and Language History*, Chapter 2 (pp.41-63) には、このような規範が hopefully の頻度にどのような影響を与えているかについての議論がある。これを読んで内容を要約し、可能であれば、他のコーパスで確認してみよう。

p.73
5 　　The key point to notice here is that virtually all the English speakers who object to the new use of *hopefully* are middle-aged or older.

　言語研究では、世代間の言語の違いを利用して、言語変化をスナップショット的に観察する方法もあり、これを社会言語学の用語を用いて、apparent time と言う。Swann, Deumert, Lillis & Mesthrie (2004), *A Dictionary of Sociolinguistics* も参照。

練習問題 70（レベル 2）
日本語について、世代間で使い方が異なると思われる事例を議論してみよう。

p.74
6 　　This project was carried out by Sarah and myself.

　ここでは、myself が普通の人称代名詞と同様に使用されている。このような文法的に必然性のない再帰代名詞は、untriggered *self*-forms と呼ばれることがあり、さまざまな英語の変種で観察されている。Siemund, Maier & Schweinberger (2012), "Reflexive and Intensive *self*-forms" を参照。

11 　　Just between you and I, Alison and Steve have broken up.

　前置詞 between に続く I は、本来ならば目的格の me となるはずであるが、いわば hypercorrection（過剰修正）によって、このように I が使用されることがある。Cochrane (2003), *Between you and I: A Little Book of Bad English* は気軽に読める興味深い

著書で、「よくない英語」について、多数の解説を含んでいる。

13　　The audience were literally glued to their seats.
　ここでの論点は、集合名詞を文法的に単数とするか複数とするかである。このような、いわゆるconcord（数の一致）についての理解を深めるには、Bauer(1994), *Watching English Change: An Introduction to the Study of Linguistic Change in Standard Englishes in the Twentieth Century* の "Concord with collective nouns"(pp.61-66)が分かりやすい。他にも、名詞の数に関する興味深い論考として、Read(1974), "Is the Name United States Singular or Plural?" と Levin(1998), "Manchester United are my Team: On Concord with Collective Nouns" を紹介したい。

練習問題 71（レベル 3）
Unit 7 で触れたように、現代英語における文法の変化については、近年多数の研究成果が発表されている。その一つ、Leech & Smith(2006), "Recent Grammatical Change in Written English 1961-1992: Some Preliminary Findings of a Comparison of American with British English" を読んで、その論点をまとめてみよう。

41　　... some people *want* to see changes which have not yet occurred. One of the most striking contemporary illustrations of this is the view of feminists who object to what they see as the built-in sexism of English and other languages.
　ジェンダーにかかわる言語変化は、意識的な変革によるものが多い。その概要はここにまとめられている通りである。ジェンダーの視点から英語を分析する研究は、Lakoff(1975), *Language and Woman's Place* 以降、急速に広がった。その他にも代表的なものとして、Tannen(1990), *You Just Don't Understand: Women and Men in Conversation* を挙げることができる。

練習問題 72（レベル 3）
英訳聖書のいくつかの異なる版、特にそのうちの一つは近年のものを選んで、ジェンダー等の観点から英語を観察してみよう。また、日本語の聖書についても、同様の観察をしてみよう。

p.76
33　　Another type of change in English which has not yet occurred but which many people have been arguing for is a rationalization of our complex spelling system ...
　英語の綴り字改革の歴史については、Unit 6、およびその注(p.108)も参照。

練習問題 73(レベル 1)
英語以外の言語についても、綴り字改革の動きがある(あった)か、調べてみよう。

p.78　Unit 14. PUTTING IT ALL TOGETHER

7　Moreover, a single language does not change everywhere in the same way. When a language is spoken over any significant stretch of territory, changes which occur in one area do not necessarily spread to other areas. As a result, with the passage of time, differences slowly but steadily accumulate among the regional varieties of the language.

特定の地域で起こった変化が、必ずしも別の地域にまで広がるとは限らない。地域方言の中に古い言語形式が残りやすいことの理由として、言語変化が及んでいないことを挙げることができる場合も多い。すでに発音の変化のところで扱った post-vocalic *r* も、その事例の一つである。Unit 5 およびその注(p.107)を参照。

12　For a while we can regard these regional varieties as merely dialects of a single language, but eventually the differences become so great that we are forced to regard the varieties as entirely distinct languages.

方言と言語の関係については、Romaine(2000), *Language in Society: An Introduction to Sociolinguistics* の "Language and dialect in Europe"(pp.11-17), "English: language and dialect"(pp.17-19), "Accent versus dialect"(pp.19-20)が分かりやすい。

p.79

41　The conquest of England by the French-speaking Normans in 1066 submerged English only temporarily; within a few generations it had re-emerged, greatly changed in its grammar and stuffed with words borrowed from French, to become in turn the national language of England, the language of the British Empire, and finally the most widely used language in the world.

ここに書かれている中英語期の英語とフランス語の関係については、Brinton & Arnovick(2017), *The English Language: A Linguistic History*(pp.241-253)の記述が簡潔で分かりやすい。

練習問題 74(レベル 3)
本書が執筆されてから今日までの間に、言語変化についての研究がさらに進み、20世紀以降の変化についてもさまざまな報告がなされている。本書では、この最近年の変化についての言及がないので、先行研究を参考にしながら、この部分を補ってみよう。すでに Unit 7、Unit 13 の注(pp.111, 125)の中で、現代英語の変化を扱った論文として Leech & Smith(2006), "Recent Grammatical Change in Written English

1961-1992: Some Preliminary Findings of a Comparison of American with British English" と Leech & Smith(2009), "Change and Constancy in Linguistic Change: How Grammatical Usage in Written English Evolved in the Period 1931-1991" を紹介したが、その他の先行研究も探してみよう。

注釈の参考文献

赤野一郎・他(編)(2015)『最新英語学・言語学用語辞典』開拓社.
Algeo, John. (1980) Where Do All the New Words Come from? *American Speech* 52: 264-277.
Bauer, Laurie. (1994) *Watching English Change: An Introduction to the Study of Linguistic Change in Standard Englishes in the Twentieth Century*. London: Longman.
Bergs, Alexander. (2005) *Social Networks and Historical Sociolinguistics: Studies in Morphosyntactic Variation in the Paston Letters (1421-1503)*. Berlin: Mouton de Gruyter.
Blake, Norman F. (ed.) (1973) *Caxton's Own Prose*. London: A. Deutsch.
Brinton, Laurel J. & Leslie K. Arnovick. (2006, 2017) *The English Language: A Linguistic History*. Oxford: Oxford University Press; 3rd edition (2017).
Burridge, Kate. (2004) *Weeds in the Garden of Words: Further Observations on the Tangled History of the English Language*. Cambridge: Cambridge University Press.
Campbell, George L. & Gareth King. (2013) *Compendium of the World's Languages, vol. 1: Abaza to Kyrgyz*. 3rd edition. London: Routledge.
Cochrane, James. (2003) *Between you and I: A Little Book of Bad English*. Cambridge: Icon Books.
Crawford, William J. (2009) The Mandative Subjunctive. In Günter Rohdenburg & Julia Schlüter (eds.), *One Language, Two Grammars? Differences between British and American English*, pp.257-276. Cambridge: Cambridge University Press.
Culpeper, Jonathan. (1997, 2015) *History of English*. London: Routledge; 3rd edition (2015).
Curzan, Anne. (2014) *Fixing English: Prescriptivism and Language History*. Cambridge: Cambridge University Press.
Davis, Norman (ed.) (1958) *Paston Letters*. Oxford: Clarendon Press.
Davis, Norman (ed.) (1971) *Paston Letters and Papers of the Fifteenth Century*. Oxford: Clarendon Press.
Davis, Norman (ed.) (2004) *Paston Letters and Papers of the Fifteenth Century*. 3 Parts. (Part

3, ed. Richard Beadle & Colin Richmond.) Published for the Early English Text Society. Oxford: Oxford University Press.

Freeborn, Dennis. (1992, 2006) *From Old English to Standard English: A Course Book in Language Variation Across Time*. London: Macmillan; 3rd edition (2006).

Gatto, Maristella. (2014) *The Web as Corpus: Theory and Practice*. London: Bloomsbury.

Horobin, Simon. (2013) *Does Spelling Matter?* Oxford: Oxford University Press.

堀田隆一(訳)(2017)サイモン・ホロビン著『スペリングの英語史』早川書房.

Howe, Darin. (2005) Negation in African American Vernacular English. In Yoko Iyeiri (ed.), *Aspects of English Negation*, pp.173-203. Amsterdam: John Benjamins.

Hundt, Marianne. (1998) It is Important that this Study (*Should*) Be Based on the Analysis of Parallel Corpora: On the Use of Mandative Subjunctive in Four Major Varieties of English. In Hans Lindquist, et al. (eds.), *The Major Varieties of English: Papers from MAVEN 97, Växjö 20-22 November 1997*, pp.159-175. Växjö: Växjö University.

家入葉子. (2019) Keith Johnson, *The History of Early English: An Activity-based Approach*. *Studies in Medieval English Language and Literature* 34: 29-34.

Johnson, Keith. (2016) *The History of Early English: An Activity-based Approach*. London: Routledge.

亀井孝・河野六郎・千野栄一(編著)(1998)『ヨーロッパの言語』三省堂.

河崎靖(2017)『ルーン文字の起源』大学書林.

Lakoff, Robin. (1975) *Language and Woman's Place*. New York: Harper & Row.

Leech, Geoffrey & Nicholas Smith. (2006) Recent Grammatical Change in Written English 1961-1992: Some Preliminary Findings of a Comparison of American with British English. In Antoinette Renouf & Andrew Kehoe (eds.), *The Changing Face of Corpus Linguistics*, pp.185-204. Amsterdam: Rodopi.

Leech, Geoffrey & Nicholas Smith. (2009) Change and Constancy in Linguistic Change: How Grammatical Usage in Written English Evolved in the Period 1931-1991. In Antoinette Renouf & Andrew Kehoe (eds.), *Corpus Linguistics: Refinements and Reassessments*, pp.173-200. Amsterdam: Rodopi.

Levin, Magnus. (1998) Manchester United are my Team: On Concord with Collective Nouns. *Moderna Språk* 92: 14-18.

Liuzza, R. M. (ed. & transl.) (2014) *Old English Poetry: An Anthology*. New York: Broadview Press.

Milroy, James. (2003) On the Role of the Speaker in Language Change. In Raymond Hickey (ed.), *Motives for Language Change*, pp.143-157. Cambridge: Cambridge University Press.

Montgomery, Michael. (1997) Making Transatlantic Connections between Varieties of English. *Journal of English Linguistics* 25: 122-141.

Nelson, Diane. (2007) Language Death. In Carmen Llamas, Louise Mullany & Peter Stockwell (eds.), *The Routledge Companion to Sociolinguistics*, pp.199-204. London: Routledge.

大沢一雄 (2012)『アングロ・サクソン年代記』朝日出版社.

Osselton, Noel E. (1984) Informal Spelling Systems in Early Modern English: 1500-1800. In Norman F. Blake & Charles Jones (eds.), *English Historical Linguistics: Studies in Development*, pp.123-137. Sheffield: Centre for English Cultural Tradition and Language, University of Sheffield.

The Oxford English Dictionary. ⟨http://www.oed.com/⟩ (2019年3月11日)

Peters, Pam. (2009) The Mandative Subjunctive in Spoken English. In Pam Peters, Peter Collins & Adam Smith (eds.), *Comparative Studies in Australian and New Zealand English: Grammar and Beyond*, pp.125-137. Amsterdam: John Benjamins.

Price, Glanville. (1998) *Encyclopedia of the Languages of Europe*. Oxford: Blackwell.

Read, Allen Walker. (1974) Is the Name United States Singular or Plural? *Names: Journal of the American Name Society* 22: 129-136.

Romaine, Suzanne. (2000) *Language in Society: An Introduction to Sociolinguistics*. 2nd edition. Oxford: Oxford University Press.

Schneider, Edgar W. (1990) The Cline of Creoleness in English-oriented Creoles and Semi-creoles of the Caribbean. *English World-Wide* 11: 79-113.

社本時子 (1999)『中世イギリスに生きたパストン家の女性たち―同家書簡集から』創元社.

Siemund, Peter, Georg Maier & Martin Schweinberger. (2012) Reflexive and Intensive *self-*forms. In Raymond Hickey (ed.), *Areal Features of the Anglophone World*, pp.409-437. Berlin: Mouton de Gruyter.

Swann, Joan, Ana Deumert, Theresa Lillis & Rajend Mesthrie. (2004) *A Dictionary of Sociolinguistics*. Edinburgh: Edinburgh University Press.

高橋博 (訳) (2008)『ベーダ英国民教会史』講談社.

Tannen, Deborah. (1990) *You Just Don't Understand: Women and Men in Conversation*. New York: Morrow.

寺澤盾 (2013)『聖書でたどる英語の歴史』大修館書店.

寺澤芳雄 (編) (2002)『英語学要語辞典』研究社.

Tottie, Gunnel. (2002) *An Introduction to American English*. Malden: Blackwell.

Trask, Robert L. (1993) *A Dictionary of Grammatical Terms in Linguistics*. London: Routledge.

Trask, Robert L. (1996) *Historical Linguistics*. London: Arnold.

Trask, Robert L. (1997) *The History of Basque*. London: Routledge.

Upton, Clive & John D. A. Widdowson. (2006) *An Atlas of English Dialects*. 2nd edition.

London: Routledge.

Wright, David (transl.) (2011) *The Canterbury Tales*. A Verse Translation by David Wright with an Introduction and Notes by Christopher Cannon. Oxford: Oxford University Press.

山口美知代 (2009)『英語の改良を夢みたイギリス人たち―綴り字改革運動史 1834-1975』開拓社.

【原著者紹介】

R. L. Trask（R・L・トラスク）

元サセックス大学言語学教授（専門　歴史言語学、バスク語）
1944 年生まれ、2004 年没
［おもな著書］
A Dictionary of Grammatical Terms in Linguistics (1993), *Historical Linguistics* (1996), *The History of Basque* (1997)

【注釈者紹介】

家入葉子（いえいり ようこ）

京都大学文学研究科教授（専門　英語学）
1964 年福岡市生まれ
［おもな著書・編書］
『文科系ストレイシープのための研究生活ガイド』（ひつじ書房、2005）、『ベーシック英語史』（ひつじ書房、2007）、『歴史社会言語学入門―社会から読み解くことばの移り変わり―』［共編著］（大修館書店、2015）

言語学テキスト叢書（原書テキスト編）
Hituzi's Linguistics Textbook Series

【第3巻】 Language Change

発行	2019年12月16日　初版1刷
定価	1700円＋税
著者	R. L. Trask
注釈者	家入葉子
発行者	松本功
装丁者	渡部文
印刷・製本所	三美印刷株式会社
発行所	株式会社 ひつじ書房
	〒112-0011 東京都文京区千石2-1-2 大和ビル2F
	Tel.03-5319-4916　Fax.03-5319-4917
	郵便振替 00120-8-142852
	toiawase@hituzi.co.jp　http://www.hituzi.co.jp/

ISBN978-4-89476-999-1

造本には充分注意しておりますが、落丁・乱丁などがございましたら、小社かお買上げ書店にておとりかえいたします。ご意見、ご感想など、小社までお寄せ下されば幸いです。

［刊行物のご案内］

文科系ストレイシープのための研究生活ガイド
家入葉子著　　定価 1,600 円＋税

英語史の研究者である著者が、自身の体験を基に書いた研究生活への道案内。論文執筆から学会参加まで、合理的な研究方法を得て知的生産活動を維持していくためのコツが満載。

文科系ストレイシープのための研究生活ガイド　心持ち編
家入葉子著　　定価 1,600 円＋税

『文科系ストレイシープのための研究生活ガイド』の続編。前著が研究人生の段階・ステップを中心としていたのに対し、どうやって研究のモチベーションを上げていくかというメンタルの側面を詳述。著者自身も抱えていたさまざまな葛藤を乗り切るための気の持ちようについて、秘伝公開。

[刊行物のご案内]

ベーシック英語史
家入葉子著　　定価 1,600 円＋税
ことばが変わっていく不思議さに焦点をあてることにより、英語史に関心を持って学べるように工夫された教科書。言語学以外のジャンルに進む学生にも面白くかつ的確にまとめられた入門書。

［刊行物のご案内］

ファンダメンタル英語史　改訂版
児馬修著　　定価 1,600 円 + 税
英語史入門書として好評の 1996 年初版を改訂。本文の加筆修正に加え、練習問題も改めた。歴史的言語変化のメカニズムを通して様々な言語学的事象への理解を深める 1 冊。